CATHOLICS
IN THE
PUBLIC
SQUARE

THE ROLE OF CATHOLICS IN AMERICAN LIFE, CULTURE, AND POLITICS

CATHOLICS
IN THE
PUBLIC
SQUARE

EDITED BY THOMAS PATRICK MELADY

MARY CUNNINGHAM AGEE • GEORGE WEIGEL • HENRY J. HYDE
ROBERT P. CASEY • ROBERT P. GEORGE • JOHN M. HAAS • DOUGLAS W. KMIEC
THOMAS P. MELADY • THOMAS S. MONAGHAN • MICHAEL NOVAK
REVEREND RICHARD JOHN NEUHAUS • THOMAS V. WYKES, JR.

Our Sunday Visitor Publishing Division
Our Sunday Visitor, Inc.
Huntington, Indiana 46750

To my first grandchild,
Alexandra Melady Morin

Previous Books by Thomas Patrick Melady

Profiles of African Leaders
The White Man's Future in Black Africa
Faces of Africa
Kenneth Kaunda of Zambia
The Revolution of Color
Western Policy and the Third World
House Divided (co-author)
Burundi: The Tragic Years
Development: Lessons for the Future (co-author)
Uganda: The Asian Exiles (co-author)
Idi Amin: Hitler in Africa (co-author)
*The Ambassador's Story: The United States and the
    Vatican in World Affairs*

TABLE OF CONTENTS

Introduction

Catholics are generally involved in the public life of the country in which they live. This is true of the Catholic community in the United States. In the early days of our Republic, Catholics were a small single-digit minority who had little or no economic power. Consequently, few Catholic laypersons were elected or served in a major national office in the first years of the Republic. The absence of political and economic power by the Catholic community was accompanied in the second half of the nineteenth century and in the first decades of the twentieth century by strong anti-Catholic prejudice.

Nonetheless, in the major geographic areas where Catholics lived — New York, Boston, Philadelphia, Chicago — Catholics, as they moved up the socio-economic ladder, also assumed a greater role in American public, cultural, and political life.

The accident of geography and the socio-political climate in the nineteenth century in the United States resulted in Catholics for over 100 years aligning themselves with the Democratic party. Most of the prominent lay names associated in that era with the Catholic social justice movement were loyal Democrats.

As the American political scene changed following World War II, Catholics entered the middle, upper-middle, and professional classes. The rosters of American educational, cultural, and civic organizations were filled with Catholics. And Catholics became more diversified in their political affiliations.

The immediate post-World War II era was a period

of general convergence between the values of most Catholics and the values of mainstream Americans. Divisions within the Catholic community itself, however, began to surface following Vatican Council II in the 1960's. There were some dire predictions about the "end of the Catholic Church."

As with similar predictions in the almost two-thousand-year history of the Church, an "end" did not happen. The Catholic Church remains alive and well.

Still, the voice of Catholicism is not as strong in this country as it could be. Many Catholics, moreover, felt in the decade of the 1980's that their traditions were being misinterpreted in the wake of the social revolution of the 1960's. Various organizations were formed to focus Catholic teachings on the contemporary social and political order. The Catholic Campaign for America (CCA), founded in 1992, was one of these organizations.

The National Committee of the Catholic Campaign for America brought together eleven leading Catholic lay persons who, before an audience of four hundred Catholic lay leaders on October 22, 1994, in Baltimore, discussed some of the leading contemporary socio-political, cultural, and philosophical challenges facing the American people.

These very important and thought-provoking talks are adapted here for our readership.

Chapter I is by Thomas Wykes, Jr., "Principles of Public Catholicism." The Executive Director of the Catholic Campaign for America shares his vision of renewal and restoration.

Mr. Wykes makes a strong case for a forceful lay Catholic voice in public affairs. And he announces his ten points of public Catholicism (see pp. 16-17). These principles, he emphasizes, are not a prescription for Catholic renewal, but a "guide for our engagement."

In Chapter II, "Catholic and American in Today's World," I give an overview of the Catholic political presence in the United States. Always a religious minority, Catholics survived great prejudice in the nineteenth century and entered the twentieth century with growing strength as a result of increasing economic opportunities in the United States.

The Catholic community currently comprises around twenty-five percent of the American population yet is faced with a new kind of prejudice. The teachings of the Church on moral issues run counter to what many citizens will accept as moral norms. I point out that American Catholics are faithful Catholics and loyal Americans. There is a renewed determination by active Catholics to advocate clearly and to campaign forcefully for their positions on significant moral and cultural matters.

Reverend Richard J. Neuhaus calls upon the Catholic community in the United States to play a strong role in strengthening the moral fiber of the country. In Chapter III, "The Catholic Moment in America," he emphatically points out that the "moment" for Catholics is here and should be seized before it passes. Father Neuhaus is President of the Institute on Religion and Public Life, a non-partisan interreligious research and education institute.

In Chapter IV, "The Call of the Second Vatican Council to the Laity," John M. Haas, John Cardinal Krol Professor of Moral Theology at St. Charles Borromeo Seminary of the Archdiocese of Philadelphia, illustrates how this "moment" for greater Catholic action is rooted in the Second Vatican Council.

United States Congressman Henry J. Hyde clearly shows the failings of our present legal interpretation of the so-called "no-establishment clause" in Chapter V, "Keeping the Promise of America." Recently named chairman of the Judiciary Committee, Congressman Hyde will continue to call our representatives to higher morals in government. This text is taken from Congressman Hyde's acceptance speech following his being named Catholic American of the Year (1994) by the Catholic Campaign for America.

The Honorable Robert P. Casey, two-term Governor of Pennsylvania, speaks from principle and personal experience in Chapter VI, "Reconciling the Faith With Public Life." Governor Casey's steadfast faith sets an example for Catholics and people of every faith.

President of the Ethics and Public Policy Center, Dr. George S. Weigel illustrates that the Catholic moment also exists in international affairs. In Chapter VII, "Catholic Citizens and U.S. Foreign Policy," Dr. Weigel urges American Catholics to apply the universal principles of human rights and religious freedom to the worldwide community.

Chapter VIII, "Preserving Religious Freedom," finds Notre Dame University's Professor Douglas W. Kmiec documenting the constitutional roots of religious freedom and the inherent rights on such matters as school choice.

Robert P. George is Professor of Legal Philosophy and Civil Liberties at Princeton University; he is also a member of the United States Commission on Civil Rights. His analysis of "Catholic Conscience and the Law" follows in Chapter IX.

The author of Chapter X, "Integrating the Faith Into a Corporate Environment," is Thomas S. Monaghan, the founder and Chairman of the Board of the world's largest pizza delivery company. This is a moving account of Mr. Monaghan's personal application of his Catholic faith to his business practices.

Mary Cunningham Agee relates her own deeply held convictions on the personal application of fundamental Catholic teachings to one's own personal life in Chapter XI, "The Emerging Catholic Voice: Integrating the Mystical Body of Christ Into the Mainstream of America." Mrs. Agee is the founder and Executive Director of the Nurturing Network, a nationwide charitable organization that provides life-supporting service to women faced with unplanned pregnancies. Like Tom Monaghan, Mrs. Agee gives excellent examples of the personal application of Catholic teachings in her life.

Chapter XII appropriately concludes this collection with theologian, author, and former Ambassador Michael Novak's reflection on "The Rediscovery of Our American Catholic Heritage." Dr. Novak's brilliant look into the past concludes with a glance at the present and the future.

Catholics in the Public Square: The Role of Catholics in American Life, Culture, and Politics is a bird's-eye view into the contemporary thinking of twelve leading Catholics.

An essential part of the American heritage is the fundamental right passed on to all Americans to advocate their beliefs in the community. This can be done in the public arena of discussion or in the advocating of legislation before city and town councils, state legislatures, and before the United States Congress. President Lincoln, for example, advocated his point of view in a series of debates.

The print media was a major avenue for the discussion of ideas and beliefs in previous decades. In today's world, modern communication includes television and radio. The phenomenon of instant communications has closed the great geographic distances between us, turning all of us into next-door neighbors. The advocacy of ideas, opinions, and beliefs is now a daily occurrence.

I hope that the beliefs, opinions, and ideas expressed in *Catholics in the Public Square* will contribute to a mature and thoughtful discussion of issues that are so important to the American people.

Thomas Melady[*]

---

[*]Publisher's note: Dr. Melady is the former U.S. Ambassador to the Vatican (1989-1993). He is also former Ambassador to Burundi and Uganda. He is President Emeritus of Sacred Heart University and the author of 12 books, including the recently published *The Ambassador's Story: The United States and the Vatican in World Affairs.*

Principles of Public Catholicism

Today we usher in a new era of "Public Catholicism." It is a day of victory, a day of new beginnings, a time for renewal and restoration.

Today we make public the lay Catholic voice in America. At a time when many are preoccupied with the darkness of dissent and a culture of death, we see the dawn of a new day.

The "Principles of Public Catholicism," presented and described here, have evolved out of a vision supported and shaped by the Catholic Campaign for America's Board of Directors. We owe each of them a debt of gratitude for their leadership.

.We must be concerned about leadership, about charting a new course for Catholic Americans. Our vision for the future is rooted in the call of the Second Vatican Council, which called upon us, the Catholic laity, to renew the temporal order and help to further the cause of Truth. It called upon Catholic laity to engage in the defense of Christian principles and their correct application to the problems of our times. It called upon Catholic laity in civic duties to promote the true common good.

In the spirit of the Second Vatican Council, we declare that now is the time for lay Catholic Americans to offer a more visible and dynamic witness of our Catholic faith. Now is the time for us to celebrate our Catholic heritage, to reaffirm our Catholic identity, to interject our own unique perspective into the public conversation. Now is the time, in this place, to this present generation to make public the lay Catholic voice in America. It is time for us to usher in a new era of "Public Catholicism."

Principles of "Public Catholicism"

I. Public Catholicism calls us to be **faithful** to the Holy Father and Magisterium of the Church.

II. Public Catholicism calls us to be **knowledgeable**, always growing in our understanding of what the Church teaches.

III. Public Catholicism calls us to **engage** the present culture with the liberating power of our faith. It calls us to offer substantive contributions to the public debate.

IV. Public Catholicism calls us to be **humble** when interjecting our perspective into the public conversation and to work with a collaborative spirit with those of other faiths. It calls us to affirm what Catholics stand for, not just what we stand against.

V. Public Catholicism calls us to be **charitable**, remembering in essentials unity, in non-essentials diversity and in all things charity — especially toward those who disagree with us.

VI. Public Catholicism calls us to be **responsible**, always sensitive to the appropriate role of the hierarchy.

VII. Public Catholicism calls us to be **consistent**, integrating our faith into every aspect of our lives. It means seeing our faith as the foundational element of our professional, family, and public lives.

VIII. Public Catholicism calls us to be **proud** of our Catholic heritage, celebrating the richness and beauty of our faith and the historic, monumental contributions that Catholic Americans have made to the cultural, spiritual, and moral life of our country.

IX. Public Catholicism calls us to be **courageous** in articulating the Church's teaching in the face of potential criticism.

X. Public Catholicism calls us to be **optimistic**, confident that our faith is capable of transforming ourselves and the contemporary culture.

These principles are not a prescription for Catholic renewal but a guide for our engagement. They are not the great painting that we, as Catholic Americans, are capable of creating; they are the framework for that masterpiece.

We are beyond hoping and waiting for renewal. It is not a matter of asking if this is "the Catholic Moment," for it is *our* Catholic moment; it is not a matter of asking do we have the leadership resources and talent to revitalize our Catholic community and transform the culture, for we do. We have made a decision and the decision is this: We will renew and revitalize our Catholic community and in the process help lead a moral restoration in America.

Renewal and restoration can only take place, however, to the extent that we dare to dream a dream of what is possible. Dare to dream the dream with us of renewal and restoration.

Now is the time for Catholic parents to instill in their children a sense of Catholic pride so that they gain a greater appreciation, a historical perspective regarding the building of the Church in America.

Catholic laity need a greater self-awareness concerning the Catholic contribution to America: our historic contributions to health care and education, the labor movement, civil rights movement, and pro-life movement. A contribution that continues today in our Catholic hospitals where fifty-eight million patients annually receive loving care. In our Catholic schools where three million students receive education with better results than public schools and at a fraction of the cost. And in our Catholic social service programs that provide open arms to teenage mothers, meals for the hungry, care for the sick, a welcome to the disenfranchised, and comfort to the dying. This is our monumental legacy of service to America.

We must never forget the heroic contributions of those who built the Church in America. Let us reintroduce our children to the great Catholic heroes. Heroes like John Carroll who founded our faith in colonial America; Mother Seton who dedicated her life to God and to the education of our children; Archbishop Fulton Sheen whose fiery evangelization converted thousands upon thousands; Walker Percy whose writings portray his great faith. Men and women who made an indelible mark on our national Catholic character.

We must never let our families forget the sacrifices of our great grandfathers and great grandmothers. People of tremendous faith who gave generously of their time, talent, and treasure — often their only nickels and dimes — to build the Catholic schools, hospitals, and institutions that benefit all of us today.

Nor can we ever forget the struggle and adversity that Catholic Americans have encountered: fighting for the right to vote and to hold public office; standing up against vicious acts of hatred and intolerance. Their example of overcoming in the midst of adversity is a bold example for Catholic Americans now when a St. Patrick's Cathedral is desecrated, when public officials unjustly criticize our bishops, or when our Church is the object of ridicule in the media. It is then when we find ourselves victims of America's most persistent prejudice — anti-Catholicism — that we should remind ourselves of the Catholic Americans who paid a great price and overcame the intolerance of their day. After all, there can be no great victory without some struggle and adversity, no Easter Sunday without Good Friday.

Now is the time for a renewal of Catholic identity. It is a time for us once again to fall in love with the richness and beauty of Church teaching. It is time for us to affirm within our families what Catholics stand for, not just what we stand against.

We stand for the right to life from the moment of conception until natural death; we stand for the permanence of marriage, the sacredness of sexuality and family as the first and vital cell of society. It is time for us to listen more attentively to the voice of our Lord, who through the holy Eucharist and the sacrament of reconciliation is drawing each of us closer to Him.

As we gain a new sense of Catholic pride and identity, we must transform the culture with the liberating power of our faith. It is not a matter of we

Catholic Americans imposing our values, but simply going on record as affirming the best values for America. It is not a matter of us demanding our rights, like an isolated interest group, but recognizing our obligation to become citizens who act in the public interest. We measure our contribution by what we bring to the table, not by what we take from it. We indeed have our own unique perspective to interject into the public conversation.

The dream of renewal and restoration is not a fantasy. There are signs everywhere that after a difficult period we are emerging from a long hard winter, and there is the smell of springtime in the air. For the skeptics who have doubts about this renewal, let them consider:

- Thousands of youth greeted the Holy Father at World Youth Day, one of the largest gatherings of young people in American history. Members of what is called generation X, tired of M-TV, walked several miles carrying crosses, and stood with tears running down their faces. For these young people, Catholic renewal was not some intellectual exercise; it had gone from their head to their heart.

- Catholic Americans rushed to their bookstores and made the *Catechism of the Catholic Church* a best-seller.

- Families are taking that catechism and instructing their children in the faith.

- Catholic universities are stimulating Catholic life. Franciscan University of Steubenville students pack the chapel for daily Mass, keep perpetual adoration before the Blessed Sacrament, and pray by a tomb for the unborn. Places like this are rebuilding the Church.

- Lay organizations like Legatus where Catholic CEO's thoughtfully reflect on how best to integrate their faith into a corporate environment are rebuilding the Church in America. These organizations are a response to men and women who are contemplating how to make the work place a holy place.

And you, the Catholic political, business, and civic leaders, all you who represent various organizations, heads of families, social organizations, you are the lay Catholic voice in America. Do you know what you are a part of?

You are part of a new emerging Catholic voice that is normal, credible, authentic, hopeful, and courageous. A voice that will usher in a new era of "Public Catholicism," a voice that will change the way Catholic Americans look at themselves and the way we are viewed by others.

Prepare yourselves for an exciting future. The time of being preoccupied with what ails us as Catholic Americans is over. The period for the greatest Catholic contribution in American history has just begun.

Catholic and American in Today's World

It is a great privilege to address my Catholic brothers and sisters from the state where Catholics first received religious freedom guarantees in the "British colonies" of the seventeenth century and where, in 1789, thirteen years after independence, the first diocese of the Catholic Church in the United States was established.

I am in Baltimore at a time of great opportunity for our country. Now, free from the distraction of major-power confrontation, the United States can dedicate its energies to promoting human rights, religious freedom, and economic development in all parts of the world.

Baltimore evokes so many good memories for American Catholics. It was here that Bishop John Carroll came after he was consecrated in England in 1790.

In the years preceding the birth of our country, John Carroll had become a good friend of the great American patriot Benjamin Franklin. The American statesman and the first leader of the Catholic Church in the United States had many fine exchanges of ideas on the government, the role of religion, and the place of spiritual values in society. Cordial discourse and mutual respect are what American Catholics wish to continue and expand in our conversations with our fellow Americans.

A Small Minority

The early Catholic Americans were a small minority — less than five percent of the total population in the early days of the Republic. While the ideal of religious freedom and full equality in the political order were among the major attractions for Catholic emigration to the United States, these freedoms did not always exist. But the ideal was there, and the United States in that period of history was one of the few countries pledged to the ideal of religious liberty.

There were departures from the noble ideals of our Constitution. Furthermore, most Catholic immigrants arrived penniless and, with the exception of the Irish and the British, few knew the English language upon arrival. But our ancestors immediately recognized that America was the land of opportunity, and they participated enthusiastically in the economic growth of our country. Our ancestors arrived with few material assets but were committed to their Catholic heritage. Their toil and sacrifice built the foundations of the American Catholic Church of today.

The political and economic turmoil in Europe in the second half of the nineteenth century resulted in vast increases in the numbers of Catholic immigrants to the United States. To the oppressed millions of European immigrants, America was the beacon light of economic opportunity and religious freedom.

It was unfortunately also a time of growing prejudice against Catholics in the United States. The literature of the time was full of highly intemperate and, in some cases, vicious characterizations of the leadership of the Catholic Church. But the immigrants continued to come in great numbers. Whatever difficulties they may have faced in the United States upon arrival were in most cases minor in comparison to the lives they had in their former "home" countries.

Despite the periodic manifestation of anti-Catholic bigotry, the Catholic Church flourished and grew in size to a double-digit percentage of the population by the end of the nineteenth century. Many new dioceses had been established including Boston, New York, Philadelphia, Newark, and Chicago. Many Catholics alive today are the grandchildren of Catholic immigrants who arrived in the great wave of the last quarter of the nineteenth century and the first decades of the twentieth century.

America was faced with its first worldwide conflict in World War I. First- and second-generation American Catholics fought in great numbers. The percentage of Catholics in the war effort exceeded the percentage of Catholics in the overall population of the country.

The relative political tranquility of the post-World War I period was broken for the Catholic community in 1927 when anti-Catholic bigotry erupted in the presidential campaign. It was a sad day for the ideals of the American political tradition. The candidacy of Alfred Smith generated a serious outbreak of anti-Catholic sentiment and agitation.

But the greatness of America was reflected in the Protestant and Jewish lay leaders who, after the elections, gathered together in 1928 and, joining with Catholics, formed the National Conference of Christians and Jews. American Catholics will always remember with grateful appreciation the decency of their fellow Americans who founded an ecumenical movement to counter religious prejudice in the United States.

Since then American Catholics have been participating in all aspects of American civic life. Now twenty-five percent of the population, Catholic Americans have seen a member of their faith, John F. Kennedy, elected president. Numerous Catholics have been appointed to positions in the cabinet and elected to high federal and state offices.

American Catholics believe in the great American dream where all Americans participate in the development of American public policy. In these circumstances, significant American public policy should reflect the best in all of the religious faith groups present in our country. Our country is a pluralistic society, and we unite with all Americans in supporting that pluralism.

Catholic Beliefs

Catholic beliefs are well known. They are rooted in Christ's teaching and in His life and in centuries of Judeo-Christian wisdom. Our teachings are set forth by those authorized by Catholic tradition to teach — the bishops of the Roman Catholic Church. And we have a universal pastor, the Pope. There should be no confusion about what Catholic teachings are. These moral values articulated by Catholic teachings have been an intrinsic part of our American culture. Our country has been respected for the importance it places on moral and ethical values.

All recent economic reports indicate how generally well the Catholic community has done economically in the United States. In appreciation for this and out of love for our tradition, we will continue our participation with Americans of all creeds in determining and affirming the moral norms that should prevail in our great country as we enter the next century.

We American Catholics have no intention of imposing our beliefs. Through advocating our centuries-old values, we expect to play a significant role in the U.S. political process that determines our country's laws. We will not be *ignored.*

The past several decades have witnessed divisions in the American civic community on important moral issues especially as they affect family values. These matters are very important to us and we intend to promote our position in order to thus influence ultimate public policy. And we make common cause with Americans of other faith traditions who concur with us on these fundamental moral issues. We look forward to working with them to maintain the moral vigor of our country.

In the past decade, there have again been manifestations of anti-Catholic bias. We have seen it in the statements of government officials and in the media. We know that this prejudice is an aberration in the American ideal which we embrace. *We have no intention of returning bigotry with bigotry.* We firmly believe that it is inappropriate for any government official to ridicule the faith beliefs of any American.

We will advocate our beliefs, always respecting other different faith-related positions. We Catholics, the past victims of bigotry, will respect the rights of others who sincerely advocate their positions on moral and family matters of concern to us all.

In the past few years, we Catholics have been offended by vulgar disturbances at our liturgical services. We know that this again is an aberration: All faith groups should be allowed to celebrate their religious services without disruptions.

These issues of morality, family, and community are best discussed in an atmosphere that is calm. Let all of us, Catholics, Protestants, Jews, Muslims, and non-believers, commit ourselves to sane and responsible expressions of opinion and action. The public square is the appropriate place for the expression of differing opinions in a dignified manner befitting the greatest democracy in the world.

There is no room in the civilized discussion of issues for shrill voices. And there is never any place for violence!

We are Catholic and American. What a beautiful gift we have received: faithful to our Church and to our country. Here in Baltimore, it is interesting to reflect on the first visit of Bishop John Carroll in 1790 when he came to assume his responsibilities as the Catholic Church leader in the United States. Then Catholics were mostly a very poor small community with no influence in our society. What a difference there is now!

Our country has given us, in these past two centuries, a home with freedom and economic opportunity. As our country faces new challenges affecting fundamental moral values, we resolve in return to work with our fellow citizens of all creeds to ensure the moral greatness of our country.

We are Catholic — faithful to the teachings of our Church — and we are Americans who love this land of freedom. What an unforgettable moment to be in Baltimore, home of the first Catholic diocese in the United States.

The Catholic Moment in America

Seven years ago I published a book, *The Catholic Moment*, in which I contended that the premier responsibility for the Christian mission rests with the Catholic Church — the premier opportunity, and therefore responsibility, for evangelization and cultural transformation in America and the world. I am regularly asked whether I think *the* Catholic Moment has been missed, whether *the* Catholic Moment is now past. The answer is emphatically *No*. I say this in part because, if the Catholic Church is what she claims to be, every moment, from Pentecost until our Lord returns in glory, is *the Catholic Moment*. I say this in part because my "reading of the signs of the times" suggests that the world is newly open to, newly hungry for, a sure word of truth and hope, a word that is most certainly possessed and most convincingly presented by the Catholic Church.

The Catholic Moment in Families

The Catholic Church offers the word of truth and hope also for the future of the family. *Familiaris Consortio*, the 1981 apostolic exhortation on the family in the modern world, declares that "Humanity's passage to the future is through the family." As reiterated in 1994's World Day of Peace Message, the Holy Father's argument is that to care about the human project is to care about the family. And the Church cares — lovingly, intensively, passionately —

about the human project, and so about the family, which today is challenged on many fronts. Indeed it may seem that the family is overwhelmed by challenges. But it all begins with, and ever comes back to, *faith* and challenges to the family.

The Church has a doctrine of the faith, a truth divinely inspired and humanly informed, regarding marriage and the family. With this truth she challenges the Catholic faithful and the world. Families that meet the challenge of faith are equipped to meet the many other challenges that will surely come their way. With faith, everything is possible; without it, all foundations rest upon shifting sand. In reflecting on family life and so much else, we are haunted by the question of our Lord, "When the Son of man comes, will he find faith on earth?" (Lk 18:8) It is no secret that the Church's teaching on sexuality, marriage, and family is ignored by many Catholics and is derided by the world. This is not to say that the teaching is rejected, for to be rejected it must be understood, and to be understood it must be taught. I trust you will not disagree if I say that all too frequently the Church's truth about marriage and the family is not taught — not confidently, not persistently, not winsomely, not with conviction.

It is not taught, in part, because in our culture it is frequently derided and distorted. Last year at the national meeting of bishops, the archbishop of Baltimore addressed with refreshing candor the ways in which the communications media are captive to a twisted version of "the Catholic story." A central component of that story is the claim that most Catholics dissent from the Church's teaching on sexuality and family life. But of course that claim is false. In order to dissent one must know what one is dissenting from. Yet that claim of the media, repeated often enough, has an intimidating and inhibiting effect upon the Catholic people, upon catechists, upon priests, and, dare I say, even upon some bishops. Repeated often enough — and it is repeated incessantly — it insinuates the suspicion that, in this vital area of human life, the effective teaching of Catholic doctrine is a losing cause, perhaps an already lost cause.

Our situation is best described not in terms of dissent but of widespread ignorance and confusion. Admittedly, the problem is compounded by the fact that there are some who do dissent — theologians and others who are not above employing ignorance and confusion in an effort to advance their own views. One speaks of this with sorrow and hesitation, and yet speak of it we must. It is not a matter of making allegations, for those responsible could hardly be more public in identifying their views and declaring their purposes. Their views are not the quiet and conscientious dissent of scholarly service to the Church, helping her to articulate the truth ever more fully and persuasively. Rather, it is all too often a dissent of bitter opposition and angry alienation. It is a dissent that confuses opinion research with the *sensus fidelium* ("consensus of the faithful") and attributes magisterial authority to "the spirit of the times" as authoritatively expressed by academic guilds and the prestige media.

This is the phenomenon addressed, no doubt with a heavy heart, by the Holy Father in the encyclical, *Veritatis Splendor*. "Dissent, in the form of carefully orchestrated protests and polemics carried on in the media, is opposed to ecclesial communion and to a correct understanding of the hierarchical constitution of the people of God." As this Pope has affirmed again and again, revealed moral doctrine is truly doctrine of the faith. What is at stake is infinitely more than intramural squabbles between liberals and conservatives, progressives and traditionalists. What is at stake is whether people understand that they are invited to the high moral drama of Christian discipleship, of living in the truth. Souls are at stake. And if we do not believe that souls are at stake, we must seriously ask ourselves what business we think we are in.

The Church has not the time, the world has not the time, countless men and women eager to live the adventure to holiness have not the time for interminable intramural disputes that obscure the splendor of Christian truth about marriage and the family. It is time to move on.

If we have the will and the wit for it, if we have the faith for it, a world that has lost its way is waiting to receive the gift of the Church, which is the good news of the One who is the Way. A world that has come to doubt the very existence of truth waits to hear from the One who is the Truth. A world falling headlong into the culture of death looks with desperate hope to the One who said, "I am the way, and the truth, and the life." (Jn 14:6) If we have the will and the wit for it, if we have the faith for it, this is our moment in *the* Catholic Moment which is every moment in time, and is most certainly this moment in time.

The Third Millennium

At the edge of the third millennium, we stand amidst the rubble of the collapsed delusions of a modernity that sought freedom and life by liberating itself from the author and end of life. Many of the best and the brightest announced the death of God; what appeared, as is now abundantly evident, is the death of man. It is for man — for the *humanum*, for men and women in their personal dignity and vocation to community — that the Church contends. The Holy Father has tirelessly reiterated that the revelation of God in Christ is both the revelation of God to man and the revelation of man to himself. Father Avery Dulles has aptly said that the teaching of John Paul II should be described as "prophetic humanism." This is the prophetic humanism that the Church proposes to a world that is wearied and wasted by false humanisms that deny both man's nature and his transcendent glory. The Church neither can nor wants to impose this authentic humanism on the contemporary world. In the words of the encyclical *Redemptoris Missio*, "The Church imposes nothing, she only proposes." But, if we understand the crisis and opportunity of our historical moment, we *will* propose the truth — urgently, winsomely, persuasively, persistently, "in season and out of season." (2 Tim 4:2)

There is reason to hope that, after the long winter of its jaded discontent, the modern world may be entering a season of greater receptivity to the truth that the Church has to offer. The great British novelist Anthony Burgess sometimes described himself as an apostate Catholic. Shortly before he died, he wrote, "My apostasy had never been perfect. I am still capable of moaning and breast-beating at my defection from, as I recognize it, the only system that makes spiritual and intellectual sense." Like the apostasy of Mr. Burgess, the apostasy of our world from Christian truth is by no means perfect. The Holy Father speaks frequently of the third millennium as a "springtime" — a springtime of evangelization, a springtime of ecumenism, a springtime of faith. He cannot know and we cannot know what is in store for us, but we can be prepared. We can be prepared to be surprised by a time in which thoughtful men and women will give a new hearing to the only truth that "makes spiritual and intellectual sense."

With respect to the family or anything else, one runs a risk by suggesting that the world needs to hear, whether it knows it or not, the truth that the Church has to offer. One runs the risk of, among other things, being accused of triumphalism. If the alternative to triumphalism is defeatism, we should not fear to be known as triumphalists. But the only triumph that we seek is the triumph already secured by the One who came "not to be served but to serve." (Mt 20:28) Springtime may not produce immediate results, indeed the result may seem like failure. But we know that "unless a grain of wheat falls into the earth and dies, it remains alone; but if it dies, it bears much fruit." (Jn 12:24) And there were seeds sown long ago in cultures once called Christian, seeds that may again be breaking through the earth that has for so long been hard frozen under the ice of indifference and unbelief. I take it that this is what the Holy Father means when he so earnestly calls us to the task of "reevangelization." To evangelize and to reevangelize — to sow anew, and to nurture to new life what is already there but has for so long been stifled and stunted by neglect and faithless distraction.

If, in anticipating the springtime of the third millennium, we are to sow more confidently and effectively, if our sowing is to transform the world (and we are called to nothing less than that!), we ourselves must be transformed. Permit me to suggest five transformations of pressing urgency. First, we need to cultivate the courage to be counter-cultural. Second, we need to appropriate more fully the gift of Peter among us, a gift luminously exemplified by this pontificate. Third, we need to recognize that the Church's teaching about sexuality, marriage, and family has a coherent structure; it is all of a piece. Fourth, we need more fully to honor marriage as a Christian vocation. Fifth, we need an intensified commitment to what *Familiaris Consortio* calls the "politics of the family."

Courage to Be Counter-Cultural

First, then, whether "in season or out of season," those who propose Christian truth must always cultivate the courage to be counter-cultural. Until our Lord returns in glory, we will be wrestling with what it means to be in the world but not of the world. The truth that the Church proposes is for the world, but the Church will inevitably appear to be against the world when the world resists the truth about itself. The necessary posture of prophetic humanism, therefore, is one of being against the world for the world. Moreover, cultural resistance to the truth has more formidable sources. With St. Paul, we never forget that "We are not contending against flesh and blood, but against the principalities, against the powers, against the world rulers of this present darkness, against the spiritual hosts of wickedness in the heavenly places." (Eph 6:12)

Especially in North America, some fear that the call to counter-cultural courage is an invitation to return to the "ghetto Catholicism" of an earlier era, but that is not the case. Sociologically speaking, immigrant Catholicism was not so much counter-cultural as sub-cultural. The progression is to move from sub-cultural striving to cultural success to counter-cultural challenge and transformation. The remarkable cultural success of American Catholics in the last half century is a tragic failure if it means that now Catholics are just like everybody else. Real success is marked by the confidence and courage to challenge the culture of which we are securely part. Or we might put it this way: There is a crucial difference between being American Catholics and being Catholic Americans. We are constantly told that there is a distinctively American way of being Catholic. The course of counter-cultural courage is to demonstrate that there is a distinctively Catholic way of being American. The Catholic Moment happens when American Catholics dare to be Catholic Americans.

An earlier generation prided itself on being accepted by American culture, and we should honor what was honorable in that achievement. But surely our task is to prepare a generation that will dare to transform American culture. Catholicism is no longer a suppliant, standing hat in hand before our cultural betters. We are full participants who unhesitatingly accept our responsibility to remedy a culture that is descending into decadence and disarray. The remedy begins with each person who hears and responds to the radical call to holiness in accord with moral truth. This is the message of *Familiaris Consortio*: "In a particular way the Church addresses the young, who are beginning their journey towards marriage and family life, for the purpose of presenting them with new horizons, helping them to discover the beauty and grandeur of the vocation to love and the service of life."

This is the message of *Veritatis Splendor*, that we are called to nothing less than moral greatness — "to be perfect as your Father is perfect." This is the drama, this is the adventure, this is the audacious hope of Christian discipleship. We must settle for nothing less, and persuade the Catholic people to settle for nothing less. We are told that young people today, immersed as they are in hedonistic self-gratification and consumerism, are deaf to the call to moral greatness. Tell that to the hundreds of thousands of young people who gathered in Denver. Tell that to millions of television viewers who witnessed in Denver a spiritual explosion in response to the culture-transforming call to live in the splendor of truth.

The Gift of Peter

The second needed transformation is for Catholics in America to more fully appropriate the gift of Peter among us as exemplified by this pontificate. For more than fifteen years now, we have been graced with one of the most determined and vigorous teaching pontificates in the two-thousand-year history of the Church. We have witnessed before our eyes the vibrant, Spirit-guided development of doctrine that John Henry Cardinal Newman celebrated as a unique strength of the Catholic Church. And yet I believe we must confess that this gift has not been truly received among us. The teaching of this pontificate, it seems to me, has hardly begun to penetrate the institutions and practices of American Catholicism. Dare I say it? In large sectors of the theological, administrative, educational, and catechetical establishments, this pontificate is viewed not as a gift but as an aberration — as a temporary interruption of the "progressive" march of intellectual and moral accommodation to the spirit of the times.

But this, too, may be changing. A younger generation is little interested in the tired ecclesiastical politics of the last quarter century, the endless wrangling of conservative vs. liberal, progressive vs. traditionalist, liberationist vs. magisterial. They want to get on with the bracing adventure of being authentically and distinctively Catholic. As for future priests, we are told that seminarians today are timorous, dull, and conformist; and no doubt there are some who fit that description. There is reason to hope, however, that there are many more who are eager to be enlisted in a great cause, to serve the greatest of causes — the salvation of souls, the daring of discipleship, the anticipation of the coming of the Kingdom of God. Pray that we will be worthy of a new generation of priests who will settle for nothing less.

Moreover, we now have, at long last, the *Catechism of the Catholic Church*. While it is addressed specifically to bishops, I hope that every bishop will make this a motto of his ministry: A copy of the *Catechism* in every Catholic home. Catholic families cannot be faithful to the teaching of the Church if they do not know the teaching of the Church. Now at last, after a long season of uncertainty, the Catholic people have in hand a reliable, lucid, and persuasive guide for living the life to which, at their best, they intuitively aspire.

The Wholeness of Faith

To cultivate the courage to be counter-cultural, to appropriate the gift of this pontificate, and then a third needed transformation: to recognize that the Church's teaching on sexuality, marriage, and family is all of a piece. Here, although we may wish otherwise, it is necessary to speak of *Humanae Vitae*. Much of the theological energy of a generation has been dissipated in rancorous dispute over that encyclical. Surely it is past time to move on. That every conjugal act should be open to the gift of new life is the consistent and emphatic teaching of at least five pontificates. Surely it is past time to acknowledge — clearly, unambiguously, and, yes, gratefully — that this is an essential part of the truth proposed by the Catholic Church. It is of a piece with all that the Church teaches about the human person in marriage and family life. That teaching is, if I may borrow a phrase, a seamless garment. A few academics may continue to fret about what is "infallible" and "irreformable," but the Catholic people cannot live well the lives to which they are called if they live with a sense of uncertainty, contingency, and conditionality about the moral truth that claims their allegiance.

Maybe, people are led to think, the Church will change its position on this or that or the other thing. The "maybes" of conditionality produce conditional Catholics, and conditional Catholics are deprived of the joy of unqualified discipleship. We are not dealing here with inconvenient rules of the Church that can be changed at will. Again *Familiaris Consortio*: "The Church is in no way the author or the arbiter of this norm. In obedience to the truth which is Christ, whose image is reflected in the nature and dignity of the human person, the Church interprets the moral norm and proposes it to all people of good will, without concealing its demands of radicality and perfection." The teaching of *Humanae Vitae*, especially as it is illuminated by the more comprehensive argument of *Veritatis Splendor*, displays an ensemble of mutually dependent insights that constitute the structure of faith regarding sexuality, marriage, and the family.

Of course there are pastoral problems, very difficult problems, in connection with this truth. The Church is infinitely patient and understanding toward those who struggle with the demands of the truth; but the Church's love is never the love that deceives by disguising the truth. The readiness to forgive is ever greater than the capacity to sin; and no one has fallen away who, having fallen, seeks the grace to rise and walk again. The People of God look more often like a bedraggled band of stumblers than a spit-and-polish company on parade, but the way of discipleship is no less splendid for that. It is the splendor of truth that calls us, and truth will not let us go.

Here, too, the teaching of the recent encyclical applies: "Commandments must not be understood as a minimum limit not to be gone beyond, but rather as a path involving a moral and spiritual journey toward perfection, at the heart of which is love." It is pitifully inadequate simply to teach that artificial contraception is wrong. In the Church's teaching, every "no" is premised upon a prior and greater "yes." All too often that "yes" has not been heard, and it has not been heard because it has not been taught. The Church's teaching is to be presented not as a prohibition but as an invitation, an invitation to what St. Paul proposed as the "more excellent way" (1 Cor 12:31) — the way of love. Only in the light of that more excellent way does the prohibition make sense. Only those who know what they are called to be can understand the commandments about what they are to do, and not to do.

The way of love is openness to the other, and openness to life. It is the uncompromised gift of the self to the other and, ultimately, to God. Against a widespread dualism that views the body as instrumental to the self, the way of love knows that the body is integral to the self. Against a sexuality in which women become objects for the satisfaction of desire, the way of love joins two persons in mutual respect and mutual duty, in which sacred bond respect turns to reverence and duty to delight. Against a culture in which sex is trivialized and degraded, the way of love invites eros to participate in nothing less than the drama of salvation.

There are many, also in the Church, who dismiss this way of love as an impossible ideal. Married couples beyond numbering who live this way of love tell us otherwise. They testify that it is ideal and it is possible. We need more effectively to enlist their testimony in advancing the authentic sexual revolution, which is the liberation of sexuality from bondage to fear of life and bondage to the self. This, too, may be part of the springtime that we are called to anticipate: that a world exhausted and disillusioned by the frenzied demands of disordered desire may be ready, even eager, to hear the truth about love. But ready or not, it is the truth that we are commissioned to propose.

Marriage Is Vocation

The fourth transformation: We need more convincingly to honor marriage and family as Christian vocation. In popular teaching and piety, it seems to me, we have yet to overcome the false pitting of celibacy against marriage. We speak of "vocations" to the priestly and religious life in a way that can obscure the truth that every Christian has a radical vocation to holiness. In agreement with a venerable tradition, we may want to say that celibacy is a "superior" calling, but we must never do so in a way that suggests that married Christians have settled for the second best. For all Christians, the greatest vocation is the vocation that is truly theirs. I expect that this truth would be more convincingly communicated were the Church to raise to the honor of the altar more Christians who exemplified outstanding holiness in their vocation as mothers, fathers, husbands, and wives. The Catholic Church has a gift for eliciting and celebrating the extraordinary in the ordinary. With respect to marriage and the family, we might do that more effectively if we had more married saints, formally acknowledged as such.

For compelling reasons — reasons freshly articulated in this pontificate — celibacy will, I believe, continue to be the norm for priests of the Latin Rite. A renewed accent on marriage as a vocation to holiness is not in tension with the vocation to priestly celibacy. On the contrary, as every Catholic is challenged to discern the radical call to live in the splendor of truth, I believe that we will experience a great increase both in vocations to the priesthood and in families that will settle for nothing less than the adventure that St. Paul describes as "being changed into his likeness from one degree of glory to another." (2 Cor 3:18)

The Rights of the Family

Fifth and finally, we need a renewed commitment to what *Familiaris Consortio* calls "the politics of the family." Years before "pro-family policy" became a popular phrase in our political culture, the Holy Father pleaded with Catholics to become "protagonists" in "family politics." He directed our attention to the Church's "Charter of Family Rights," and urged upon us the rich doctrine of "subsidiarity" which underscores the importance of mediating structures in society and, above all, the irreplaceable role of the family. No state, no party, no academic institution, no other community of faith has proposed such a comprehensive and compelling vision of the family in the modern world. The Church's teaching is a bold proposal for family justice that can inform public thought and action on everything from welfare policy and employment practices to the right of parents to choose the education they want for their children. School choice is not a matter of preference but a matter of justice. For the poor among us, it is increasingly a matter of survival.

And, of course, family rights presuppose the most primordial of rights, the right to life. To strike at the transmission of life is to strike at the heart of the family. Here, however inadequately, the Catholic Church has already had a transformative influence on American culture. Although today, thank God, we have many allies, especially among Evangelical Protestants, for a long time Catholics stood almost alone in the witness for life. Without the Catholic Church there would be no pro-life movement in America or the world today. The proponents of abortion, euthanasia, population control, and genetic engineering are right to view the Catholic Church as the chief obstacle to their ambitions. We earnestly pray that one day they may be persuaded to be our friends, but until then we wear their enmity as a badge of honor.

We will not rest, nor will we give others rest, until every unborn child is a child protected in law and welcomed in life. We do not deceive ourselves about the encircling gloom of the culture of death. Perhaps the darkness will grow still deeper, but we will not despair. We have not the right to despair, and, finally, we have not the reason to despair. For we know that the light of life shines in the darkness "and the darkness has not overcome it." (Jn 1:5) The darkness shall never overcome it. Never. Never.

"Humanity's passage to the future is through the family." The prophetic humanism of this Pope and this Church proposes to the Catholic people and to the world how that future can be lived with moral dignity and grandeur. We do not know how this proposal will be received, but we will persist in proposing it "in season and out of season." At the edge of the third millennium maybe the springtime is at hand; maybe the long dark winter has just begun. We do not know. We do not need to know. God knows.

We do know this: Now is the time of our testing. And it is the time of our splendor in contending for the splendor of the truth. If we have the will and the wit for it. If we have the faith for it.

The Call of the
Second Vatican Council to the Laity

A Disordered Society in Need of Redemption

My oldest son drove me to his university in Philadelphia one day through a decaying part of the city. Driving along streets strewn with trash, we passed blackened shells of once quaint homes and apartments. Pointing out old townhouses with every doorway and window filled with concrete block and mortar, he informed me that they had been "crackhouses." After the police raided such houses, they were sealed up like tombs to prevent them from ever being used again. As we drove along, we saw men lifting brown paper bags to their lips as they lounged on cluttered steps and in filthy doorways. The bags, I learned, contained liquor bottles to help the men in their relentless pursuit of oblivion. My son recounted the day a gunfight broke out on roof tops above him while he sat at a red light. I was horrified at sights my son had come to see as commonplace.

That early morning drive was terribly unsettling and led me to ponder just how advanced was the decay in our society. The family itself seems to be disintegrating. The number of children born out of wedlock increases every year. What were supposed to be lifelong unions between husband and wife are dissolved with increasing ease as one state after another permits "no-fault" divorce. Venereal diseases are at their highest incidence since the end of the

Second World War. Our nation's capital has become also its murder capital with most killings related to drug trafficking.

More than a quarter of a century ago, the Fathers of the Second Vatican Council met to assess the role of the Church in the modern world. They noted that the situation in the world was dire. They were meeting at a critical moment in history, "At a time" the Fathers said, "when grave errors aiming at undermining religion, the moral order and human society itself are rampant." Those words were uttered before the so-called "gay-rights" movement and the public desecration of a sacred host by some of this movement's adherents. They were written before anyone had ever heard of AIDS. They were written before the legalization of abortion in the United States and the efforts of the current administration to export the practice worldwide. They were written before pornography had burgeoned into a multi-billion-dollar-a-year industry the U.S. They were written before a committee of the National Institutes for Health had issued recommendations for guidelines for bringing about human life in a test-tube for purposes of experimentation and then destruction.

If the Council Fathers thought the situation bleak in their own day, they would be horrified at what would confront them today. The Council Fathers knew what the solution to the problems of their day had to be. And they told us. The fact that the situation has grown continually worse in the intervening years suggests that we have not clearly understood the Council's prescription for remedying the situation. After referring to the grave errors undermining religion, the moral order, and human society, the

Fathers declared that "the Council earnestly exhorts the laity to take a more active part . . . in the explanation and defense of Christian principles and in the correct application of them to the problems of our time."

Call to the Laity

The action which the Council Fathers proposed for the restoration of the social order was that lay people be thoroughly, completely, unapologetically, clearly, and enthusiastically — lay. That is, that they fulfill their own unique vocation within the Body of Christ.

And the role of the laity in the Body of Christ is to be secular. In fact, this is what distinguishes them in the Church. We read in the conciliar "Decree on the Apostolate of the Laity" that *the* characteristic of the lay state is "a life led in the midst of the world and of secular affairs."[1]

In the conciliar "Dogmatic Constitution on the Church" we read that "by reason of their special vocation it belongs to the laity to seek the kingdom of God by engaging in temporal affairs and directing them according to God's will. . . . There they are called by God that . . . they may contribute to the sanctification of the world, as from within like leaven, by fulfilling their own particular duties."[2] We are actually to seek our salvation "by engaging in temporal affairs and directing them according to God's will."

Well before the Second Vatican Council, Pope Pius XII had spoken of the laity as the primary means for correcting the errors of society. The Pope addressed the cardinals in 1946:

> The faithful, and more especially the laity, are in
> the front line of the Church's life; it is through them

that she is the vital element of human society. In consequence they, they above all, ought to have an ever more clear consciousness, not only of belonging to the Church but of being the Church, that is, the community of the faithful on earth under the guidance of its common head, the pope, and of the bishops in communion with him.[3]

Pius XII reminded us laity that we do not merely belong to the Church, we *are* the Church every bit as much as the hierarchy is the Church. We may *belong* to a Saturday night bowling league, but we *are* the Church. We may *belong* to the local country club or health club, but we *are* the Church.

His Holiness Pope Paul VI picked up the Council's vision of the laity in his encyclical *Populorum Progressio*. The Pope wrote: ". . . it belongs to the laymen . . . to take the initiative freely and to infuse a Christian spirit into the mentality, customs, laws and structures of the community in which they live."[4]

I had invited a friend to a function of the Catholic Campaign for America on one occasion but he declined saying that the Campaign would go nowhere if the "red hats" were not leading the way. The "red hats" were of course the cardinals. But Paul VI, speaking in the spirit of the Second Vatican Council, did not tell us laity to wait for the "red hats." He said "it belongs to the layman . . . to take the initiative freely. . . ."

Autonomy of the Secular Order

The Catholic Church teaches that there is a certain autonomy to the secular order where we lay people find ourselves which is appropriate to it even as it is ordered toward God, the ultimate source and goal of all that is. The Council Fathers tell us that "All that goes to make up the temporal order: personal and family values, culture, economic interests, the trades and professions, institutions of the political community, international relations, and so on, as well as their gradual development — all these are not merely helps to man's last end; they possess a value of their own, placed in them by God."[5]

When John Paul II at his inaugural Mass told the world, "Do not be afraid of Jesus Christ!", he meant it. He urged the world to open its doors and windows to Christ, for the Church respects the autonomy and unique character of temporal institutions. As Catholics we believe that grace perfects and elevates nature. It does not destroy it. As a consequence, Catholics will only enhance all that is already good and noble in the temporal order while eliminating all those things which pose a threat to human dignity.

The Council Fathers tell us that "Laymen ought to take on themselves as their distinctive task (the) renewal of the temporal order."[6] But they are to do it from within, as leaven in the bread.[7] One of the dangers inherent in some public Catholic movements is that they look as though we Catholics are setting ourselves over against society. But that, of course, is not the case. We are society. We are inescapably members of society, and as we are transformed, society will be transformed from within. The only way in which the temporal order *can be* renewed is when there are well-formed Catholics serving as effective senators or representatives in Congress, as television executives, as movie producers, as journalists, as attorneys, judges, and Supreme Court justices, doing their jobs extremely well in accord with the professional standards of their respective callings and with unfailing fidelity to the moral law of God.

There is no short-cut to the transformation of the temporal order. And as we transform it by growing personally in holiness, we must respect it for what it is. As the Council Fathers said, "Far from depriving the temporal order of its autonomy, of its specific ends, of its own laws, and resources, or its importance for human well-being, this design [of leaven in the loaf], on the contrary, increases [the temporal order's] energy and excellence, raising it at the same time to the level of man's integral vocation here below."[8]

We Catholic laity are not to deceive our co-workers in the American Bar Association or the American Medical Association, for example, by making them think that we are one of them when we really are not, so that we can more effectively infiltrate the organizations and take them over. Quite the contrary. We are inescapably one with our co-workers and must attempt to be the best attorneys or doctors or whatever we can be in accord with the recognized standards of our own profession in so far as they conform to the moral law.

A Catholic stockbroker is not being a good stockbroker, or a good Catholic, if he says he will simply allow the Holy Spirit to pick out the best stocks for his clients each morning by choosing those which his eyes first encounter when he opens the paper. He is a good Catholic stockbroker if he researches stocks well and knows the needs of his clients and what will be best for their portfolio. Catholicism recognizes an appropriate autonomy to the secular order. The rules on stock options are the same for Christians as they are for Jews.

No one in the world need fear Catholicism will try to impose itself on the world. It respects the autonomy of the secular order.

Secularism: an Inappropriate Autonomy

There is, however, an inappropriate autonomy, a presumed independence of the secular order from the supernatural, which goes under the name of secularism. In his "Apostolic Exhortation on the Role of the Laity," Pope John Paul II asked: "How can one not notice the ever-growing existence of religious indifference and atheism in its more varied forms, particularly in its perhaps most widespread form of secularism?"[9]

This secularism argues that social life can be ordered without any reference to the supernatural, to the transcendent, to God, the author and judge of all. This approach to the social order wants to shape society as though there were no God. As the Council Fathers solemnly warn us: ". . . just as it must be recognized that the terrestrial city, rightly concerned with secular affairs, is governed by its own principles, thus also the ominous doctrine which seeks to build society with no regard for religion . . . is rightly to be rejected."[10]

This attitude of secularism, a kind of atheism the Pope tells us, is deadly, quite literally deadly. It has led to the undermining of commonly accepted norms of morality to such a degree that social life now faces varying degrees of disintegration. Under the cultural hegemony of secularism, millions of the unborn have been slain, and voices now clamor for physician-assisted suicide. Under the cultural hegemony of secularism and its denial of objective moral norms, tens of thousands now languish from AIDS, a condition arising principally through immoral practices.

The secularist state, no longer able to acknowledge a Creator God, can now no longer even define what constitutes the basic unit of society, the family. When we were still a religious nation, we could recognize that the family had a specific make-up, granted to it by God Himself. But once God has been banished from public life, the state becomes the final arbiter of what reality is. The state will decide what a family is, whether it be two homosexual men with an adopted child or two lesbians, one of whom has been artificially inseminated. If there is no God, there is no intelligible created order. As the Fathers of the Second Vatican Council said, "Without the Creator, the creature himself becomes unintelligible."

Secularism is a plague, a curse, upon our society, the remedy to which lies in the teaching of the Second Vatican Council of a *true* secularity, subject to an objective moral order, informed and shaped by divine grace. As the Council taught us, "The secular character is properly and particularly that of the lay faithful."[11]

Laity Are Consecrated People

After stressing the secularity of the laity, it might be surprising to find the Council teaching emphatically that the laity must also be understood as "consecrated" people. They have been called out from the world, consecrated and set apart by the waters of baptism.

Consecration means "to be made holy with." Of course, God alone is Holy. But through our baptism, we are made one with the Holy One of Israel. In baptism we are consecrated, that is, made holy with Christ Jesus, God incarnate. Since we have become one with Him, we are to live His life in the world, which was a life *for the world*. As members of the Body of Christ, we are to share in His redemption of the world! It is only through us, the members of His Body, that Christ is able to bring salvation to the world. As the Council Fathers tell us: "Since he wishes to continue his witness and his service through the laity also, the supreme and eternal priest, Christ Jesus, vivifies them with his spirit and ceaselessly impels them to accomplish every good and perfect work."[12]

But the laity share in the redemptive work of Christ according to their own nature within His Body. They are to share in Christ's redemptive work in the world as lay people, by virtue of their baptismal consecration. But there is another consecration in the Church, ordination to holy orders. By this consecration, men are set apart for the service of the altar, they are conformed sacramentally more intensely to the priestly life of Christ and are empowered to offer the holy Sacrifice of the Mass. They are so configured to Christ, that they live as He did. Just as Jesus, they have forsaken wives and children and home life so that they can give themselves entirely to our service as we live in the world.

This priestly consecration does not apply to lay persons, of course. Nor would lay persons want any of the responsibilities or privileges attached to that vocation since it is not their own. The lay Christian consecrated through baptism is, quite specifically in his secularity, to bring into the midst of the world the very life of Christ Himself. No one but the lay Christian can truly do it.

The Council Fathers recognized that the lay Christian was immersed in the daily life of the world and that it was therefore his task to transform it. In the decree on the apostolate of the laity, the Fathers speak of "the apostolate of like to like." The priest cannot be everywhere. He is not expected to be. But the Christian laity are, literally, everywhere. The priest cannot be all things. The Christian laity are. Salesman. Nurse. Secretary. Research chemist. Farmer. Forest ranger. Real estate agent. Fighter pilot. Dance instructor. Computer programmer. Psychiatrist. Policeman. Through the apostolate of like to like, we laity witness to our own. And that witness is far more effective than it would be if it came from a priest or religious because we can "speak to our own," knowing their concerns, their trials, their triumphs within their work or family life.

The priest cleanses us from our sin and feeds us with the Food of Immortality so that we may more effectively carry on the work of transforming society.

Through the sacraments we become conformed to Christ in His service to the world. And as we imitate Him we must remember that the vast majority of our Lord's redemptive life was living as a tradesman, a carpenter in a Palestinian village in the midst of a family. Our Lord's saving act did not take place simply on Calvary. True, His entire life was ordered toward that sublime moment, but He began to bring about our redemption from the moment He was conceived in the womb of Mary. His ordinary, "secular" life was also redemptive. We must keep this in mind and try to see our normal, everyday, secular activities as also redemptive as we carry them out as members of the Body of Christ.

Consequently the *hidden* life of Jesus offers itself to us as a model for the life of the lay Christian which the Council called on us to lead. And Christ's hidden life was unexceptional. It escaped notice. And herein lies, I believe, one of the most remarkable characteristics of our religion.

We Catholics worship as God a man who labored at a work bench for most of His life with only a brief public ministry crowned with an ignominious death. When our Lord did begin His public ministry and began performing miracles, the neighbors could respond only with perplexity and incredulity: "Is not this the carpenter, the son of Mary and brother of James and Joses and Judas and Simon, and are not his sisters here with us?"[13] Consequently those who imitate Jesus Christ will follow Him in their hidden life as parent or tradesman or professional. This naturally calls for a certain anonymity — in imitation of Christ.

Anonymity of course does not mean not having a public impact. Quite the contrary. How many could name the script writer for their favorite soap opera or situation comedy? Yet look at the profound public impact these anonymous figures have. Our anonymity in Christ means that our first responsibility is to work quietly and well at our own given task. It means that we seek salvation through our daily work, whether it be as an employee for a public utility or a Supreme Court Justice. If one does his work faithfully with a deep love of God, imbuing it with the grace of Christ, it will have its public impact.

The Council Fathers speak of this pervasive work of the laity, most of which will receive no public notice, but all of which will be effective for the transformation of society. "And so," the Fathers write, "worshipping everywhere by their holy action, the laity consecrate the world itself to God."[14] Remarkably the Fathers here are not speaking of devotional activities in church. They are speaking of the daily tasks of Christians in the world as they are united to Christ on Calvary through the Eucharist. Consequently, our most mundane tasks become, according to the Fathers, "holy actions" through which the world itself is consecrated to God.

Quietly, persistently, by doing one's immediate duties well out of love for God, the Christian will begin to transform society from within. Only then will there be a public Catholicism which is truly effective because it will be shaped by saints. The public manifestation of the faith arises almost spontaneously from a religious people. To transform society, we must first convert souls, one at a time, where we find them in the work place, the board room, the supermarket.

Just how radical this teaching of the Council is can be seen in the difficulty with which it has been understood and implemented in the post-conciliar period in the life of the Church. We hear unceasingly of the laity having come into their own within the Church; we hear of the Church of the emerging laity; we hear of the great influence of lay ministries.

However, it is regrettable that the enhanced role of the laity is seen today almost exclusively in terms of the laity becoming more involved in the institutional life of the Church. Laity now fill the sanctuary as lectors and cantors and extraordinary ministers of the Eucharist. Here we see the tendency, which still exists, to understand a committed Christian life in terms of the clerical life. It is assumed that the more the laity come to be like the priests, the more they are viewed as truly committed Catholics.

There is nothing wrong with these ministries but they are far removed from the role of the laity envisioned by the Second Vatican Council. The Council told us that the laity "are hidden with Christ in God. . . . Generously they exert all their energies in extending God's kingdom, in making the Christian spirit a vital, energizing force in the *temporal sphere*."[15] Our proper place as laity is in the temporal order. And no one should be able to intimidate us from fulfilling our God-given vocation by insisting that we keep our Catholic selves confined to the four walls of a church or the privacy of our own homes.

However, the world is not simply the context for the Catholic to live out his Christian vocation but becomes the very substance of his Christian life. In his apostolic exhortation on the laity the Holy Father tells us that: "The *world* . . . becomes the place and the means for the lay faithful to fulfill their Christian vocation, because the world itself is destined to glorify God the Father in Christ."[16] The world, including the public forum, has been redeemed by Christ and so has been turned over to the lay Christian to be remade and transformed according to the Mind of Christ — indeed in His image. And this is *our* God-given task and joyous privilege as lay Catholics.

The Fathers of the Second Vatican Council tell us that the way by which the laity seek the kingdom of God is specifically "by engaging in temporal affairs and ordering them to the plan of God."[17] Now it is just such assertions which the secularist will find offensive. The question will be posed: "In a society in which there is no established religion, how can one segment of the population presume to take on the task of ordering temporal affairs according to the plan of God?"

Of course, we Catholics believe that we have a clearer idea of God's plan for temporal society because of what has been revealed in Jesus Christ. But as Catholics we also believe that the created order reflects the mind of God so that any person of right reason and good will, even a non-ideological secularist, can perceive what will most benefit humanity and what will do it harm. Even those who do not acknowledge Christ should be able to see the plan of God revealed in the natural law. As St. Paul teaches us in Romans: No one has an excuse for not knowing the law of God in the most fundamental matters of human conduct.

There should be a certain fundamental moral order so that redemption can be facilitated. The Council Fathers tell us that we ought to so order the structures of society that they serve as inducements to virtue and not to sin. They write:

> . . . by uniting their forces, let the laity so remedy the institutions and conditions of the world when the latter are an inducement to sin, that these may be conformed to the norms of justice, favoring rather than hindering the practice of virtue. By so doing they will impregnate culture and human works with a moral value. In this way the field of the world is better prepared for the seed of the divine word and the doors of the Church are opened more widely through which the message of peace may enter the world.[18]

The Need for Sanctification

Although our religion is intensely personal, it cannot be privatized. Man is a social animal, and his beliefs and practices will inevitably have a social expression.

One thing I am certain the Council Fathers never envisioned nor desired was the disappearance of what I call the "public Catholicism of the common man." I remember riding a streetcar as a young man in downtown Pittsburgh. All of a sudden a number of men in the car tipped their hats while others crossed themselves. I was totally perplexed as to what gave rise to this odd behavior. When I inquired of my father, he asked what streetcar route I had taken. When I told him, he responded, "Oh, that car goes in front of Old St. Mary's Church. Those men were Catholics. They do that sort of thing when they pass by a church." I now know that those common, ordinary men in streetcars in downtown Pittsburgh were acknowledging our Lord in the Blessed Sacrament in the tabernacle of the church as we rode by.

There was also the odd sight of the women working in the cafeteria of the public school I attended all coming to work once a year with a black smudge on their foreheads. I learned that they were Roman Catholics, and the dirt had something to do with a religious observance at the beginning of Lent! I now know that they had attended Mass on Ash Wednesday and were acknowledging publicly that they were sinners, that they had come from dust and were going to return to dust, and that they placed their only hope in Jesus Christ.

I remember the huge, barrel-chested foreman of the ditch-digging crew of the gas company I worked for over the summers while I was in college. He was as tough and fearsome a man as I had ever encountered, and I remember him turning on a man in the ditch one time with a pointed finger and a stern warning, "Hey, bud, we don't use that kind of language around here!" I learned that the foreman was a member of the Holy Name Society, a group of Catholic men who had pledged themselves to defend the Holy Name of Jesus whenever it was profaned. These were real men, courageous men, who came to the defense of the Holy Name not only at home around the dinner table, but also on the factory floor, in the ditches, on the assembly line. This was "public Catholicism" at its best —simple, direct, guileless, courageous. These were men who would come to the defense of their Church and of their Lord as spontaneously and as swiftly as they would come to the defense of their mothers or wives or daughters.

The task of transforming culture from within belongs quite specifically to the laity in their secularity. The task is urgent and requires first of all sanctity, holiness, on the part of the lay faithful. Unless there is interior growth in holiness all else is useless effort. Catholics can attend a function of Catholic Campaign for America once a week, but if they are not becoming increasingly transformed according to the mind of Christ, the effort will do them no good. The Blessed Josemaria Escrivá said that if one did not act with sanctifying grace, he was accomplishing as much as a seamstress sewing with her needle but without thread. There is activity but nothing is being accomplished.

Also, the task of transforming society will be generational. The process of secularization has proceeded for centuries. It will take generations to reverse its deadly effects. This is an age and a culture in need of redemption. But the sanctification of culture can be achieved only in and through a sanctified laity.

And there is no better school for training in holiness than the Catholic family. As John Paul II has pointed out in his apostolic exhortation on the laity, the family has "the task of being the primary place of 'humanization' for the person and society."[19] And God knows we must humanize our present society. Earlier in the same document he had said: "The lay faithful's duty to society primarily begins in marriage and in the family. This duty can only be fulfilled adequately with the conviction of the unique and irreplaceable value that the family has in the development of society and the church itself. The family is the basic cell of society. It is the cradle of life and love. . . ."

I have no idea what means God will employ to be the primary agency for the preservation of Catholic truth in these dark ages we have entered upon and to assist in the building of a new civilization of love in the future. But, I cannot help but think that it may indeed be the Catholic family. I think that this may also be the mind of our current pontiff, for no Pope in history has written so much on the family or expressed such concern for its well-being. It was fundamentally his love for the family which drove him to international confrontations over the Cairo Conference. It is from the family that we will have our future legislators and journalists and playwrights and business executives and priests and religious sisters. There, surely, is the cradle of life and love which can ultimately affect the re-evangelization of culture and its transformation into a new and unique expression of God's love. It is through the Catholic family surely that our faith will have its most profound impact in the public arena.

Notes

1. *Apostolicam Actuositatem*, 2.
2. *Lumen Gentium*, 31.
3. "Address to the College of Cardinals," February 20, 1946, A,A,S, 1946, p. 149.
4. *Populorum Progressio*, 48.
5. *Apostolicam Actuositatem*, 7.
6. Ibid.
7. See *Lumen Gentium*, 31.
8. Ibid.
9. *Christifideles Laici*, 4.
10. *Lumen Gentium*, 37.
11. *Lumen Gentium*, 31.
12. *Lumen Gentium*, 33.
13. Mark 6:3.
14. *Lumen Gentium*, 34.
15. *Apostolicam Actuositatem*, 4.
16. *Christifideles Laici*, 15. Emphasis added.
17. *Lumen Gentium*, 31.
18. *Lumen Gentium*, 36.
19. *Christifidelis Laici*, 40.

Keeping the Promise of America

Hard as it may be to believe, it was ten years ago that Cardinal O'Connor launched the Great Church/State Debate of 1984 by reminding a Catholic candidate for the second highest public office in the land that the Church's teaching on the morality of abortion was ancient, consistent, unalterable, and binding on the consciences of all Catholics. Moreover, the Cardinal argued, that teaching was entirely consistent with the great American tradition, enshrined in the pledge of allegiance to the flag, of "liberty and justice for all." The abortion license defined by the Supreme Court in *Roe vs. Wade* was not, therefore, simply an offense against Catholic morals; it broke the promise of America. It coarsened and debased our public life. It threatened the moral integrity of the American democratic experiment.

But Cardinal O'Connor surely proved the truth of Mark Twain's remark that "No good deed goes unpunished." And we want to thank Your Eminence (the cardinal) both for the good deed and for bearing the subsequent punishment so nobly. What would the *New York Times* have done without Cardinal O'Connor to flagellate for the last ten years? On advice of counsel I won't even speculate!

The debate the cardinal started in New York quickly moved to the American heartland, and the governor of New York accepted the invitation of Notre Dame University's Theology Department and visited South Bend to sort things out in this troublesome business of church and state. He didn't succeed in that, I fear, but he at least succeeded in provoking an invitation to me from Notre Dame's Law School to respond to him. There, I tried to clear up some of the confusion that had turned what should have been a serious reexamination of the first principles of our constitutional order into something of a sound bite media circus. For nothing less was at stake here, I believed, than the place of religion and religiously-based moral values in American public life.

A Religious Character

At Notre Dame ten years ago I noted, for instance, that Walter Mondale's claim that religious conviction in America had always been "intensely private . . . between the individual and God" was historically bizarre. As I said then, that would have "come as news to John Winthrop and the pilgrims, to Jonathan Edwards, to the Abolitionists, to Lincoln, to fifteen generations of the Black church, and not least to American Catholics taught by the magisterial John Courtney Murray, architect of the (Second) Vatican Council's 'Declaration of Religious Freedom.' "

And I am happy to say that, whatever else has happened over the past ten years, that argument seems to have struck home. For despite the continuing hysteria in the elite culture and the prestige press, most Americans have come to understand that what Father Neuhaus has called the "naked public square" — the systemic stripping of religion and religiously-based moral values from American public life — is profoundly undemocratic, given the undeniably religiously character of our people.

The welcome accorded to Yale law professor Stephen Carter's recent book, *The Culture of Disbelief*, with its sharp criticism of the imposition of official secularism in our law and politics, is one sign of the times from which we should take heart. So, too, is the bipartisan enactment of the Religious Freedom Restoration Act, which was both an important achievement in itself and, just possibly, a small step away from the confusion that the Supreme Court has created over the past fifty years by subordinating "free exercise" to "no establishment" in its First Amendment jurisprudence.

There is, to be sure, a long way to go on this front. And until the Court recognizes the truly bizarre nature of its attempt to "balance" two "religion clauses" — when in fact there is only one "religion clause," in which "no establishment" is the means to the end of "free exercise" — we will continue to flounder in a lot of confusion. But let us hope that, as I say, a first step back towards constitutional common sense has been taken. Permit me, too, a brief comment on which has been the occasion for so much comment, not least from the Oval Office. As I understand Stephen Carter's argument, he recognizes that Americans continue to be a deeply religious people (Carter himself is a serious Christian, which perhaps makes him something of an anthropological curiosity at the Yale Law School). He deplores the public impact of the Supreme Court's religion clause jurisprudence, which he believes has created a bias toward secularism in our law and politics, and he suggests that we should reorient our thinking toward what might be termed (in my words, not his) the "maximum feasible accommodation" of religion in American public life.

While welcoming the first two of Professor Carter's assertions, I think we must decline to applaud the third. What we want, and what the Constitution requires, is not "accommodation." Nor will it do to settle for "toleration." No, the free and public exercise of religious conviction is not to be "tolerated": It is to be accepted, welcomed, even celebrated as the first of freedoms and the foundation of any serious scheme of human rights. And until that notion has gotten itself recemented back into the foundation of American public life, we will continue to experience the tacit establishment of secularism in our law and our politics.

Refuse Catholic Bias

What might Catholics in America do to help move the country back toward a recognition of the crucial importance of biblical norms and values in public life? What can we do, as Catholics, to help reclothe the naked public square?

The first thing we can do is to refuse to accept the anti-Catholic bias that is epidemic in the American academy, the prestige press, and the popular entertainment industry. It is scandalous that Catholic belief and practice can be mocked and pilloried by editorial writers, TV sit-coms, movies, Broadway shows, rock and rap groups, with virtually no sustained, public response from Catholic Americans. We have got to recover our self-respect. We have got to recover our nerve. We belong here. We don't have to take this kind of thing quietly anymore. The revitalization of the Catholic League for Religious and Civil Rights and the creation of the Catholic Campaign for America, are two welcome signs that Catholic

Americans are rousing themselves to the defense of the Church and the defense of democratic civility in America.

For that is precisely what is at stake here. We know that the gates of hell will not prevail against the Church, so we need not worry about the ultimate victory of Hollywood. But we had better worry about an America in which one-quarter of the population is subjected to public ridicule because of its most deeply held beliefs. For that is an America in which the foundations of civility have eroded dangerously.

Be Catholic Americans

The second thing we have to do, as an American Catholic community, is to liberate ourselves from the mythology of John F. Kennedy's Houston campaign speech in 1960. That speech, according to conventional wisdom, emancipated Catholic Americans for full participation in American public life. The sad truth of the matter is that that speech was the prelude to the naked public square. For what did Senator Kennedy do? He argued that no religious institution (which presumably means, no set of religious convictions) should have a direct or indirect influence on public policy in the United States of America.

Kennedy's Houston speech, like his 1962 commencement address at Yale, suggested that an America "come of age" had no real need of such old-fashioned sources of moral wisdom as religious conviction and classical moral philosophy. No, this was the age of "rational decision-making" by technocrats who understood that the real problems of the late twentieth century were technical and managerial, not substantive.

Tell them that in the South Bronx. Tell them that in south central Los Angeles. Tell that to the young woman struggling with the crisis pregnancy. Tell that to the youngster trying to learn to read in a school that he enters through a metal detector so that his classmates can be disarmed. Tell that to the cops policing neighborhoods where children shoot children over basketball shoes, or hustle crack cocaine. Tell them that America's problems today are technical and managerial.

One of the things that has happened over the past ten years, since Governor Cuomo and I spoke at Notre Dame, is that things have gotten far worse than we imagined possible then. There are entire parts of our cities where to walk down the sidewalk is to risk your life, and the human tragedy of that situation, the tremendous loss of lives that could otherwise be creatively lived, scars our minds and offends America's conscience. And because of that, there is an opening, a window of opportunity, to remind America that character counts; that democracy depends, in the final analysis, on the virtues of a people and that a revitalization of biblical faith, not technocratic reason, is the most likely way to rekindle virtue in the American republic.

Catholic Americans could help drive that message home; but we won't, until we disentangle ourselves from the mythology of the Houston speech.

Challenge Religious Leadership

The third thing that lay Catholics can do is to challenge our religious leadership to an ever more vigorous public defense of the moral law in our public life. Many of us are in the arena, whether by vigorous participation in public life, or, God and the electorate willing, in public office. We intend to stay there! We don't expect and we don't want priests and bishops to be politicians. We do expect and want them to be religious and moral teachers, and to be that publicly.

In my state of Illinois, one of the prominent candidates for the Democratic nomination for governor is a Catholic who is busily running around the state making sure that the people of Illinois understand that he is militantly pro-choice. In the state of Maryland, two of the prominent candidates for the Democratic nomination for governor are practicing Catholics. Each is vying to assure the voters, especially in the Washington suburbs, that he is more pro-choice than she is, or vice-versa.

The list is depressingly long of prominent Catholic politicians who have consciously turned their backs on the defenseless pre-born for the modern-day equivalent of thirty pieces of silver. Some of them even get invited to Catholic universities to be honored or to deliver important speeches. This widespread betrayal of the pre-born makes all the more luminous the heroism of Governor Bob Casey of Pennsylvania. The passivity of so many of our Church leaders in the face of this abandonment of principle is easier to explain that it is to justify.

My point is not that the bishops, or the Catholic conferences of these and many other states, should be out on the stump, declaiming against candidates for public office. My point is that the bishops have to exercise their teaching authority by making two things clear, time and again, in and out of season, through all the instruments of public persuasion at their disposal.

First, the bishops have to make clear that the Catholic defense of the right-to-life of the unborn is not an optional part of some mythical Catholic consumer package. Second, the bishops must make clear that Catholic defense of the right-to-life of the unborn is not a matter of sectarian dogma, but rather a position grounded in a natural-law ethic. Which is to say, it is a position in defense of civil rights, in defense of a hospitable American society, in defense of the American promise of justice for any member of the human family, regardless of social status, race, gender, or accident of birth. These things have not been made sufficiently clear over the past ten years, despite the intense efforts of leaders like Cardinal O'Connor. We have to make them clear today. And our bishops have to help us keep the issue alive, precisely as the great civil rights issue of our day.

The Holy Father has shown us all how this can be successfully done in his magnificent encyclical on the moral life, *Veritatis Splendor*. For, the carping from the usual suspects notwithstanding, the encyclical has been warmly welcomed in the United States, with over a hundred thousand copies having been sold so far. Why has this happened? Because more Americans than we may think have finally figured out that the crisis of America today is a crisis of character, and that it can only be resolved through a reinvigorated public moral culture.

Our bishops thus have a splendid opportunity to seize a "Catholic moment" in our national life and to fill the American yearning for moral seriousness with real content. We want them to do that. We need them to do that.

And if they do that, they will not find the rest of us wanting. I believe that there is a great, latent hunger for leadership in American Catholicism, just as there is in America in general. Working together, bishops, priests, religious, and lay Catholics can realize for our time Lincoln's promise of a new birth of freedom.

That, and nothing less than that, is the challenge that the times have laid before us. There is so much to be done, and in the words of St. Paul, "now is the acceptable time!"

Reconciling the Faith With Public Life

Recently, a very distinguished person whom I have had the occasion to meet, Father Wilson D. Miscamble, chairman of the history department at Notre Dame, wrote a piece that I think should be required reading for those of us who are engaged in the mission of bringing our faith into public life. He issued a challenge, a call really, for renewed political activism addressed to ". . . [T]hose Catholics who believe that their church's teachings — on respect for human life, on concern for the common good, on responsibilities as well as individual rights, . . . and on the importance of family and community — have something important to contribute to American political life."

That call, it seems to me, has particular relevance and resonance to our mission of renewing the temporal order.

When you merely recite those teachings, it calls to mind the teachings of our country's founding fathers: the experience of our country, working out over time its destiny as a very unique country, which claims for itself a higher calling, a calling dedicated to a societal concern for the less fortunate, and to a recognition of the inherent dignity of every person. That's who we claim to be.

I want to explore Father Miscamble's challenge and the contribution that he thinks we can make against the backdrop of my own experience as a public official.

Demands of Conscience

As I see it, the obligation of a public official is to do what he thinks is right, to follow his own conscience, whether that conscience is formed by religious faith, experience, the natural law, common sense, or all of the above, as is most often the case.

We've got to first put the challenge in a familiar context to all of us.

Today, we see in the national liberal and conservative policies of our country a temptation to ignore the serious demands of conscience, to abdicate responsibilities for others and acquiesce in a breakdown of our sense of community, the common good, and respect for human life.

It seems to me that both ends of the spectrum tend to fall prey to different sets of temptations.

Many conservatives seem to close their eyes to the common good and social responsibility, as I view it. I am talking about our obligation to the less fortunate, to the poor, to the sick, to the unemployed, to the homeless, to all of those people in our society who perhaps need a helping hand. And who among us — let's level with each other — who among us has not, at some time in his or her life needed a helping hand, from family or friends? None of us, I suspect, has escaped because that's the human condition — no matter who we are.

And yet for Catholics, this challenge of finding a true social responsibility still stands. Doesn't it? It's more powerful today perhaps than any time in our history. You start with *Rerum Novarum* of Leo XIII and go down to *Sollicitudo Rei Socialis* of John Paul II. The Church has consistently stressed the obligation, *obligation*, to work for social justice, for the common good, by fighting for life and balancing rights with responsibilities, working to strengthen family and community, and helping the poor.

Consider, for example, these words which I just recently had occasion to read. How striking they are. Some would even say radical. Let me read them to you. They are the words of St. John Chrysostom quoted in the new *Catechism of the Catholic Church*, so it has a contemporary relevance. Here's what St. John said: "Not to enable the poor to share in our goods is to steal from them and deprive them of life. The goods we possess are not ours, but theirs."

Now try that one on for size. Think about it. Strong words. Powerful words. And yet they cannot be ignored by those who would offer distinctively Catholic contributions to America's political discourse. Because just as our country lays claim to a unique role for itself, so also do we as Catholics lay claim to a unique role in American life for ourselves.

How many times have you heard the expression or the statement from those who are not Catholic: "I can't believe that he or she did that because, you know, he's a Catholic." Even our bitterest enemies somehow concede to us — as our mission — something above and beyond, something different, something unique, something distinctive, something driven by a higher purpose. They take us at our word, which is appropriate.

When we talk about human life, we say to our country: America, we take you at your word. We've read the Declaration of Independence, and we believe it. We don't believe for a minute that that Declaration can be repealed by a Supreme Court which seeks to change the rules of the natural law as they apply to the dignity of every human person. So, we're different, and our country is different.

For me the challenge is not reconciliation between the different philosophies. I think they are incredibly consistent, remarkably consistent. That's what I would like to leave with you today and, in a sense maybe, challenge or contradict the title of my remarks. As I thought about coming here today, I never had a conflict in my own mind. It's been an extension of who I am and what I believe, and I've always tried to act that way as a public official.

Basic Responsibilities

We have a basic responsibility for the less fortunate among us. It is a societal responsibility without any question. But I believe government has a necessary role to play in this process. I am not one of those who says, "Let the devil take the hind-most, and the race belongs to the swift and the strong. Those that can't keep up, well, that's unfortunate, but that's none of my business. It's a tragic circumstance, and we feel deeply and badly about it, but that's too bad. We must stand aside."

For only the second time in our history — think about this — we've abandoned an entire class of people. Only once before — you know the familiar analogy from the 1850's and 1860's, the Dred Scott era — have we done this. For the second time in our history, we've abandoned an entire social class. I'm talking about the unborn child. We've said, despite what it says in the Declaration of Independence, despite whom we claim to be as Americans, there's nothing we can do. The children must die.

That's un-American. We've never done that before in our history. That's why I bridle every time somebody says to me that the issue of human life is a merely Catholic issue. They try to pigeonhole us and say this is a Catholic issue.

Of course it's a Catholic issue. But it's much more than that, because in this country the consensus on this issue — we've had a consistent consensus historically — has been a secular consensus, and a national consensus, and a popular consensus, driven by the people. A consensus with which most organized religions happen to agree, thank God. Don't ever let them say that the position of the United States of America before 1973, before that aberration called *Roe vs. Wade*, was anything but a secular consensus, subscribed to by believers and by non-believers.

If you want to see diversity, which is a very fashionable word, go to the state legislatures of this country, and you will see diversity with a capital D, with all kinds of people, men and women, believers and non-believers. And it was their consensus which said, "The taking of innocent human life is a felony, is a crime." It was that secular consensus that was transformed with the stroke of a pen in 1973 into a constitutional right. That's why this country has been acting as though it has a bone in its throat. It can't accommodate that kind of dislocation. It was never meant to accommodate that kind of dislocation. That's also why ultimately we're going to prevail. Abortion is un-American in its essence.

I can't read this off of a page. We've got to bring passion to this cause, and we can't let the passion cool. We can never lose our sense of outrage. That's what it takes: "outrage." We've got to say to ourselves and to the people of this country, "How can they do this to America?"

I've often said, if we could go back in our mind's eye to the turnstiles at Ellis Island — because we are all children of immigrants; I hope that never becomes a cliche, because it happens to be true — if we went back to the turnstiles at Ellis Island and said to those people coming through the turnstiles, wide-eyed and thrilled to be in a free country for the first time, "Let me tell you something. I'm going to tell you something that I'm going to ask you to comment on. You're coming now to America, and America is a country which gives less protection to the unborn child than any civilized society in the world — less protection." What would they have said? I think they would have said, "Now wait a minute. You can't be talking about America. Maybe you're talking about some other country. Maybe you're talking about the country we just left. Not in America. That can't be."

This issue has real power. They talk about hot-button issues. This is *the* hot-button issue. This is going across this country — in my judgment, this and related issues — like a tidal wave and somebody's going to ride that wave. And there are people now getting in the way of that wave. Are there not? They are going to be swept aside. They are going to be flushed out of the system. They are going to lose power, because the only thing we can do is take the power away from them. You see, it's either them or us. It's as simple as that.

We have an obligation to those less fortunate. We've tried to meet that in Pennsylvania:

We have provided free health insurance for poor

children and low-cost insurance for the children of the working poor.

We have provided jobs for our people by working actively with the private sector. We have the largest state economic development budget in the nation. Nothing affirms the basic dignity of each person more directly than the feeling of self-worth and fulfillment which only a job can provide.

We have had a strong and consistent pro-family agenda, and backed it up with financial commitments in our state budget at a time of declining revenues caused by the worst recession in recent memory.

We have some of the best health, child care, and nutrition programs in the country for women, children, and families.

We created the Statewide Adoption Network, making adoption a state priority for the first time in our state's history.

We've crafted residential drug treatment programs so chemically-dependent mothers do not have to relinquish their children in order to get treatment. Governmental policies should keep families together, not drive them apart.

We've cut income taxes for poor families and families of the working poor four times, bringing financial relief to many struggling families.

We are working to change perverse, anti-family disincentives in the welfare laws which discourage marriage and work and encourage teenage single parents to live apart from their parents.

We've doubled funding for our state scholarship programs to bring a good college education within the reach of more young Pennsylvanians.

We have supported family and medical leave to enable family members to care for sick relatives.

We have championed new and expanded programs to help and protect the elderly.

Sure, you can have debates about the respective role of government versus individual contribution and community responsibility. What we can't deny is the common responsibility that we all share.

Right and Wrong

That's the conservative side of the ledger. When you look at the liberal side, you find deficiencies that are just as serious. You see a breakdown in responsibility and community and emphasis on rights to the exclusion of corresponding responsibilities.

License is favored over liberty. Rights are emphasized, responsibilities are ignored. Relativism is rampant, ignoring the fundamental and changeless absolute — in some quarters today what I'm about to say is heresy, but I'm going to say it, because it's true — the fundamental and changeless absolute that there always have been, there are now, and there always will be things that are right and things that are wrong. There's a temptation out there among those that espouse the liberal social justice agenda to fall prey to the whole package. We must resist that, and I'm speaking of myself as well as of others who feel as I do. We cannot go on in silence with their cultural agenda which runs contrary to our most basic values.

As a nation, we are only now waking up to the false and empty promises of liberation held out by abortion-on-demand and no-fault divorce. We have the fruits of those "brilliant" ideas. The feminization of poverty, psychological trauma, juvenile crime, teenage suicide. Life is very cheap, isn't it? And people wonder why.

Mother Teresa told us, didn't she, when she visited Washington recently: How can we have 1.6 million unborn children killed every year and then talk about the tragedy of children shooting children on our streets? It just doesn't compute. It's of a piece. It's the same basic problem, disrespect for human life.

So we see these twin tendencies at work: an indifference to private responsibility on one hand and an indifference to social responsibility on the other. Their advocates, it seems to me, are saying that as a society we can't do any better than just simply leaving each other alone. But that's not what America is supposed to be all about.

I believe America is better than that. I know it's better than that. And so do you. And our history confirms it. We've got to be clear on our mission. The unborn child is at the center of the cultural debate. It's the most important social question, the most compelling and far-reaching civil rights issue. It never gets put into those terms. That's exactly what it is: the most important and far-reaching civil rights issue of our time. If ever there was a time for the Catholics of America to live up to this challenge by being faithful to their beliefs and faithful to the traditions of America, this is the time, and this is the issue.

I see the legalization of abortion as a rejection of the American experience. America was born with a calling, the noblest calling, the noblest destiny, to which any society can be called. Thinkers like George Weigel and Robert George have eloquently stated that our national history has been the story of inclusion, of extending rights and opportunities, of defending the powerless, of widening the circle of the commonly protected. To me, protecting the unborn child follows naturally from everything I know about my country. Abortion can have no legitimate place in American life. Nothing could be more foreign to the American experience. It is inconsistent with our national character — with all that we've done, with everything we hope to be.

We have those public officials who say that they are personally opposed to abortion but in their public position they're not going to reflect that attitude because to do so would be forcing their views on others. It seems to me the only reason for a public official to advertise private opinions or religious beliefs about abortion, when they have no bearing on the public position of that official, is to make a cynical appeal for support from pro-life voters.

I think at this point we've got to call to mind the words of Thomas More in the wonderful play *A Man for All Seasons* when he said: "I believe, when statesmen forsake their own private consciences for the sake of their public duties . . . they lead their country by a short route to chaos." You can't have two consciences — one private, and one public — one at work and the other at home. It cannot be right to do publicly what you know, in the privacy of conscience, to be wrong.

The question to ask public officials is not whether they adhere to private religious beliefs. The question to ask is: What are you going to do in your public position and in your public policies about the human carnage of abortion in our society?

It is easy to let people put this out of mind. We can't see the victims. They don't vote. They don't have any names. No political action committee's down there patrolling the halls of Congress when the Freedom of Choice Act is on the agenda. They're faceless. I've often said I wished that I could have met some of those twenty-seven million kids that never got a chance to be born. I would liked to have met some of them. I would liked to have benefitted from their idealism, and their energy, and their brilliance, and their strength. You talk about wasted assets. God help us. It's mind-boggling. It defies comprehension to even think about it.

We've got to remember that, because we're talking about America's children. We're not talking about Somalia, Rwanda, or Bosnia, however, horrible those pictures have been. We're talking about America's children who are being denied the chance to be born. We've got to be vocal. We can't be accomplices in silence. We can't pretend it's just another issue among a laundry list of issues. That's another cop-out, where it gets equated with a lot of other things that are important but don't rise to the cosmic importance of the protection of human life.

An abortion is very different than almost anything else we confront today. It's not a victimless crime. It is direct, deliberate, violent injustice that makes an equally direct demand upon the consciences of those who recognize it as such. And beyond recognizing it for what it is, for the evil that it is, we've got to go one step further. We've got to do something about it. We're burdened with the knowledge of the evil that it is and because we are who we claim to be, American Catholics, *American* Catholics.

We have an obligation to be who we claim to be. To fulfill the mandate imposed on us by our self-declaration of what we claim is important to us. So we have an affirmative obligation to work to protect innocent human life. I'm talking about political activity, ladies and gentlemen. Let's get right down to it. The only relevant activity is political activity in a democracy, because that is how you change things. Otherwise, it's just a nice, great big debating society. Let's get right to the nub of this. I think that's where it is, in my judgment.

Signs of Hope

You know today is a day not only for challenges, but for optimism.

As America faces the monumental challenge of legalized abortion, signs of hope are everywhere. You couldn't tell by reading the popular press or by turning on your television for the six o'clock news, but signs of hope are everywhere.

Without question, there's something fundamental and dramatic stirring across the heartland of this country. It's that wave I've talked about that's palpable — you can feel it. If you're in politics and you can't feel that wave, you're in the wrong business. You ought to be selling life insurance or doing something else, but you shouldn't be in politics, because it's there. You can taste it. And I think the people on the other side are beginning to taste it too. Beginning to feel it. Beginning to feel the hot breath of the people. Because character is important. Values are important, and people care about them. They vote that way, thank God. Without question, something dramatic is happening. We're witnesses to what I think is a revolution. Something which gives me great hope and confidence for the future is quietly and slowly and painfully but inexorably changing. Like the Dred Scott situation, inexorably, legal abortion cannot stand. We spit it out of our mouth. We cannot swallow it.

Inexorably, the American people are coming to the conclusion that we cannot live with abortion. Consider the signs: the Freedom of Choice Act. Tom Foley said, "lead pipe cinch, you can't miss." Oh yeah? Down in flames — failed.

Eighty-three percent of the counties of America have no abortion clinics. You know why? Because the people don't want them there. That's why.

Only thirteen percent of public hospitals will perform abortions. Fewer and fewer medical schools — consider this — are teaching abortion. Most doctors will not touch it with a ten-foot pole. That's why when President Clinton — it got in one paper, *USA Today* — lifted the ban on abortion at U.S. military bases overseas, with much fanfare, every single American military doctor in Europe and Asia refused to participate in the abortion procedure. Everywhere.

That's why we're here today, joined in common cause and the firm conviction that in America every child deserves a chance to be born.

What is called for now is very simple. It's a theme of this conference. It's called leadership. Moral leadership of a high order. Gutsy leadership. Tough leadership that doesn't back down. That keeps punching and keeps fighting and keeps persevering until the end is reached over time, as it will be. But leadership also with a strong dimension of generosity and understanding, sending a message of civility and respect for opposing views, a message that bespeaks a true sense of community.

Leadership which presents the protection of the unborn child for what it truly is — an imperative that flows naturally from the historic social justice mission of America. You've got to continue to carry this message until it's reflected in the laws and the policies of our nation, as one day it surely will be. Until we are once again a caring community that offers women solid alternatives to abortion and offers children and families the help that they need to have a real chance to live decent, happy, and healthy lives.

There is no doubt that this country faces a crisis of awesome dimensions. There is equally no doubt that we will ultimately prevail.

In responding to the crisis, we've got to put our best hope for the future where we've always placed it: in the common sense and basic goodness of the American people.

There is no need to wait for political consensus. It's already formed. It's here, and it grows every time someone looks at a sonogram. All we need are leaders, not apologists to soothe us into inaction — those people waiting for the so-called "consensus" to form, and then when it forms, run out in front of the parade and lead the parade. We don't need people like that. They're a dime a dozen. They diagnosis the problem; they don't have the guts to do anything about it. We need leaders who work for change — who *work* for change, *CHANGE* here and now.

Today, in the spirit of great hope and great optimism, I bring this challenge to you.

I ask you: If those leaders are not to be found among those gathered here today, where will they be found?

Catholic Citizens and U.S. Foreign Policy

"How many divisions has the pope?" That derisive question was first posed by Josef Stalin, and he got his answer in the 1980's when the Pope and the Pope's divisions led the revolution of conscience that made possible the nonviolent overthrow of Stalin's empire in the collapse of European communism.

But others, too, have derisively asked, "How many divisions has the Pope?" International Planned Parenthood and its allies in the U.N. bureaucracy and the U.S. State Department didn't worry about the Pope and the Pope's divisions when they tried to make the recent international conference on population at Cairo enforce the sexual revolution through international law and foreign aid programs. But a funny thing happened on the way to Cairo: the Pope and the Pope's divisions began to say *No*, and to say *Yes*.

The Pope and the Pope's divisions said *No* to the idea that people are pollution.

The Pope and the Pope's divisions said *Yes* to the dignity of every human life from conception until natural death.

The Pope and the Pope's divisions said *No* to abortion-on-demand as an internationally-recognized human right.

The Pope and the Pope's divisions said *Yes* to the special life-giving and life-affirming vocation of women.

The Pope and the Pope's divisions said *No* to the abuse of women by men who treat women as mere objects for their manipulation and pleasure.

The Pope and the Pope's divisions said *Yes* to better education, better health care, and more effective legal protection for women, and *Yes* to service to women in crisis.

And that powerful message of moral conviction — that bold and unapologetic *Yes* to the gift of life — turned the tide at Cairo and frustrated the schemes of International Planned Parenthood, the U.N. Fund for Population Activities, and the Honorable Timothy Wirth, Undersecretary of State for Global Affairs.

So, it turns out that the Pope has lots of divisions. Indeed, it turns out that John Paul II, this providential Bishop of Rome, is the most powerful voice in the world speaking on defense of basic human rights and defending human rights on the basis of a universal moral law.

We should be proud and humbly grateful to be counted among this great Pope's divisions.

The question for us now is, how do we live out our Catholic vocation — the primary commitment of our lives — as citizens of the United States, the world's lone, and sometimes lonely, superpower? How do we help make the lone superpower the responsible superpower?

I have two suggestions: one in the order of issues, international diplomacy, and citizen activism; the other in the order of ideas and national self-understanding.

Religious Freedom

First, and on the issues side of things, we should recall that one of the central themes of the social doctrine of John Paul II has been that religious freedom is the first of human rights, the foundation of any meaningful scheme of human rights, and the keystone of a genuine democracy.

This is a theme with a deep resonance in the American Catholic experience. The colony of Maryland was founded in part as a religious refuge for Catholics forbidden the public practice of their faith in England. In the city of Baltimore (my hometown), Archbishop John Carroll, the founder of the American episcopate, lived religious freedom; James Cardinal Gibbons defended the American arrangement as compatible with Catholic understandings of the just society; and Lawrence Cardinal Shehan helped bring the American experience of religious freedom and toleration to fruition in the life of the universal Church at the Second Vatican Council.

I would simply point out that the struggle for religious freedom continues around the world, even after the European communist breakdown. The Church, today, Catholic and Protestant, is being persecuted in China, Vietnam, and North Korea. There are great difficulties in the Islamic world, especially in the Middle East. There is a terrible persecution going on in Sudan, including the enslavement of adults and the selling of children. Christian leaders from various Protestant communions were assassinated in Iran in 1994.

American Catholics should help keep the spotlight of attention focused brightly and sharply on these places, and indeed wherever men and women are persecuted on the basis of religious conviction.

There are special opportunities now, in the Peoples Republic of China (where the "most favored nation" issue has been resolved) and in Vietnam (with which the administration has resumed trade); in both of these situations, American investment and business is sure to play a large role in determining the future evolution of society. Will American Catholic business leaders help that evolution include a considerable measure of moral and cultural transformation, toward the ends of religious freedom? We should certainly hope that that's the case.

Finally, on this front, may I commend to you the work of the Puebla Institute, a lay Catholic organization working on behalf of religious freedom for all, and ably led by Nina Shea, one of the country's most dedicated, respected, and reliable human rights attorneys. She is a model of the kind of engaged Catholic citizen so desperately needed in our society today.

The Need for Morality

Second, and on the idea side of things, we all understand that "national interest" is the phrase of the moment in foreign policy debate. Roman Catholics have to insist that defining the "national interest" is as much an exercise in moral reasoning as it is in political, economic, or diplomatic calculation.

For as the philosopher and diplomat Charles Frankel once wrote, the heart of the decision-making process is not finding the best way to serve a "national interest" that we already know and understand; the heart of the decision-making process is *determining what that "interest" is* — assessing our resources, needs, commitments, traditions, and aspirations — determining, in short, our national calendar of values.

There is no "amoral" politics. All politics, even international politics, engages unavoidable moral issues. Aristotle understood, over two millennia ago, that politics was an extension of ethics. We should do the same, today. John Paul II bids us to help create a civilization of solidarity and love. We should help direct American energies toward that task.

In debating the "national interest," then, we are debating not only what America should and shouldn't try to do in the world; we're debating *who we are* as a people, and *what we want to stand for* in the world. And in that debate we have no surer guide, no wiser counselor, than the Pope of freedom, John Paul II.

Preserving Religious Freedom

John Courtney Murray wrote thirty years ago:

> The question is sometimes raised, whether
> Catholicism is compatible with American democracy.
> The question is invalid as well as impertinent; for the
> manner of its position inverts the order of values. It
> must, of course, be turned round to read, whether
> American democracy is compatible with Catholicism.

How do we answer this question? Do we hide our
faith and its social teaching in embarrassment or for
fear of giving offense?

If we do, I submit we understand neither American
democracy nor Catholicism.

Indeed, I contend that the central organizing
principle of Catholicism lies at the very core of the
American Republic. I am, of course, not speaking here
in a denominational sense. The founders of our nation
— Jefferson and Madison in particular — rebelled
against any notion of coerced belief or practice. The
oppression of religious taxes and religious oaths to own
property or to vote or to hold office led to the historic
remonstrances for religious freedom by these great
historical figures. They led to the enshrinement of the
value of religious liberty in the words of the First
Amendment that "Congress shall make no law
respecting an establishment of religion or prohibiting
the free exercise thereof." But a commitment to
religious freedom in no way entails the denial of the
affirmation of a Creator God in the Declaration of

Independence. The words of the First Amendment were not intended to exclude God from our lives, but to ensure that reason could be guided by faith — the only kind of faith worth having, premised upon free will, not force.

Reason guided by faith. This is the natural law tradition of Augustine, Aquinas, Maritain, Murray, and John Paul II. Reason guided by faith. This is the natural law tradition of Thomas Jefferson who secured the American cause in the Declaration of Independence upon "self-evident truths" derived from the "law of Nature and Nature's God."

Yes, Murray was right: To ask whether Catholicism is consistent with American democracy is impertinent and inverted. It reveals an ignorance of, in the words of the late Russell Kirk, "the roots of the American order." These roots extend deep into the natural law tradition of the Catholic faith as well as that of the Hebrews, Greeks, Romans, the scholars of the medieval world, and the reformation.

Think about it. The law of the Hebrew prophets was indeed prophetic of our modern society. If we listen to this revealed word, we are given cautions against all the ills graphically displayed on the nightly news: horrible violence, corruption, selfishness and materialism, hypocrisy, and an eroding complacency in the face of it all. The Hebrews taught us that social order is premised on law, but that the law will only be effective if it is founded upon — as Cicero wrote centuries before Christ — "the highest reason, implanted in Nature."

Natural Law

It was Cicero who reminded us that it is the "most foolish notion of all" to think that "the principles of Justice [are] found on the decrees of peoples, the edicts of princes, or the decisions of judges." If law merely had to be declared to be valid, Cicero wrote, "it could sanction robbery and adultery." But the positive law has not this power. The law cannot transform evil into good. And no matter how many times the Supreme Court mandates it, nor how many times our President and his wife declare it, the law — the natural law — cannot, and does not, sanction the murder of innocent human life.

As St. Augustine instructs: The state's function is to constrain man's sinful appetites — the greed, the lust for unbridled power, and in this, the state can keep the peace. But that peace is destroyed if the state forces us to worship false gods, including the most imposing of those false gods, the state itself. Aquinas, building on Aristotle acknowledges that the state can be a source of common good, and we must obey the law of the state to avoid scandal. But the secular law must not bind in conscience if it is contrary to the natural law, and it does not bind at all, if it contradicts God's divine law.

Our legal system, of course, inherited English common law. But even this more immediate ancestor is best understood as derived from Hebrew law and Christian morality. Here we find the Magna Carta and the English Bill of Rights putting the King, and later parliament, squarely under the law that God has written in our hearts.

As Catholics, as Catholic Americans, in a campaign to restore America to the truth of her history and the aspirations of her destiny, preserving religious freedom means everything. As Tocqueville — in many ways the first objective observer of the American scene — so astutely observed, religious faith is vital to the continued strength of America. Listen to his words:

> [The American people] all differ in respect to the worship which is due the Creator; but they all agree in respect to the duties which are due from man to man. Each sect adores the Deity in its own peculiar manner, but all sects preach the same moral law in the name of God. . . . Religion in America takes no direct part in the government of society, but it must be regarded as the first of their political institutions; for if it does not impart a taste for freedom, it facilitates the use of it. . . . How is it possible that society should escape destruction if the moral tie is not strengthened in proportion as the political tie is relaxed?

How, indeed? Do our public schools strengthen this moral tie? You know the answer before I give it. The answer is in the ever-climbing rates of teen pregnancy. The answer is the staggering rates of student violence and in the guns that populate school lockers that once held books. In my home state of Michigan, a select committee was appointed to evaluate the state's model curriculum. This is what it found: "the curriculum advances moral relativism"; "it falls short in supporting families and family values"; children who object to this moral skepticism "are sent to sit in the principal's office, with miscreants who had broken school rules. Many were put in the hall and held up to open ridicule by the teacher and fellow students." The report concluded: "[the public] schools are trying to educate our children and young adults with only the most superficial and questionable attempts to develop their characters and their moral values."

If the answer that is given to this sorry tale is that the public schools can do no better because the Constitution erects a wall of separation between church and state, then the answer is wrong. How can a Constitution framed by individuals who prayed at every turn for God's guidance and inspiration be read to expel God from the classroom and public discussion? How can an American Republic founded on "the law of Nature and Nature's God" survive if it denies God and insists upon destroying its own nature? American Catholics are called by their faith and their love of country to oppose massive health care plans that will use coercively raised tax money to destroy life. American Catholics are called by their faith and love of country to reject opinions like that of the Colorado Supreme Court which deny its citizens the ability to draw reasonable moral distinctions between those individuals who are committed to maintain the integrity and social order of sexual relations between husband and wife and those who are not. American Catholics are called by their faith and love of country to steadfastly deny the effrontery and inhumanity of a medical doctor who thumbs his nose at his state's criminal law by killing off people in a van parked at the curb.

Restoring the Original Intent

If the First Amendment is to be properly understood, it must be given its original understanding. And that is quite simple and direct: two different clauses — the free exercise clause and the establishment clause — and one purpose, the freedom of religion. The free exercise clause was intended to promote religious freedom by making sure that the government did not prohibit religious practice or belief. If my religion requires me to drink sacramental wine, the government cannot prohibit its consumption. Of course, if I had a religious practice that required me to do grave harm, the state could step in to preserve human life and public order, but not otherwise. Just as the government cannot prohibit religious belief and practice under the free exercise clause, on the establishment side, it may not prescribe or dictate religious belief or practice under coercion of law or threat of penalty.

That's it. That's the original understanding of the religion clauses. These clauses do not say that public busses transporting children to or from private schools are okay, but not busses for field trips. These clauses do not say that the public provision of secular textbooks are okay, but not maps or remedial teachers of math and grammar working in the context of a private religious school. These clauses do not preclude voluntary prayer and certainly not a voluntary moment of silence. These clauses do not preclude the balanced teaching of God's creation along with the theory of the Big Bang. These clauses do not prevent the state of New York from accommodating the needs of handicapped children merely because they are Hasidic Jews living within the same village. And most importantly, these clauses do not deny the objective morality derived from the immutable, created essence of human nature or inhibit in any way the robust discussion and reliance upon religious revelation of all denominations in order to better understand that nature.

But, of course, what the religion clauses say and

what the Supreme Court of the United States says they say are two different things. On the free exercise clause, the court has taken the position in the last few years that generally applicable neutral prohibitions, including prohibitions of religious practices, are acceptable just so long as the government does not specifically intend to stamp out the religious practice or single it out for disfavor. Thus, if temperance and the Prohibition era returns, the use of sacramental wine in a religious liturgy can be precluded as easily as the drinking of wine out of a paper bag in the back seat of a car. Under this strange judicial construction of the free exercise clause, if we as Catholics need an exemption to practice our religion, we will have to write our congressman.

Apparently, a number of Catholics — and those of many other religious denominations as well — did write their congressmen because that national assembly has purported to "reverse" the court with the passage of the Religious Freedom Restoration Act. Now, substantively, the act may well be a good thing, but it poses a dilemma in the constitutional order. How exactly — constitutionally speaking — Congress can reverse the Supreme Court is a bit problematic. It is especially troublesome for American Catholics because, wouldn't you know it, this very same purported congressional authority is relied upon by proponents of the so-called Freedom of Choice Act, to preempt even the meager ability of states to protect the unborn that was grudgingly acknowledged in *Casey vs. Planned Parenthood* (1992).

The past thirty years of establishment clause cases are no better, and perhaps, worse. A clause intended to prevent government coercion of belief or practice has been transformed into a clause that mindlessly and aggressively excludes religion. Exclusion and noncoercion are not the same. Exclusion, under the Court's so-called *Lemon* standard (aptly named) means every public act or program must be free of all but meaningless ceremonial references to God. The original and correct noncoercion standard, by contrast, affirms free will — the freedom of each individual to accept or reject God without the heavy hand of government penalty. As Jefferson said, the true understanding of religious freedom under law is that "it neither picks my pocket nor breaks my leg."

Denying Religious Heritage

Are legs broken or pockets picked when the Knights of Columbus get a permit to erect a nativity scene on the city hall steps? To ask the question is to answer it — except that is for the Supreme Court, who directed that such nativity scene be taken down. Religious symbols and references are only permitted by the court if they are surrounded by a sufficient number of distracting secular symbols or drained of all religious meaning. And the federal exclusion of religion from the public square has now spawned a second level of state exclusion and denial of religious heritage. For most of this century, a simple cross has stood atop Mount Soledad in San Diego. Under California's highly exclusionary "no preference" clause in its state constitution, a judge has ordered this cross hauled down.

To its credit, the city of San Diego sought to accommodate religion by the simple expedient of selling the fifteen-foot-square area beneath the cross to a not-for-profit private foundation. But even this accommodation is claimed by the Society of Separationists to be an establishment of religion because it would "privatize the Constitution." On this reasoning, San Diego better hope the separationists do not remember that San Diego, translated from the Spanish, invokes the memory of Saint James. The constitutional guarantee of religious freedom is being turned inside out. And the exclusion of religion from public discussion inextricably leads to the state as religion. It is the advent of totalitarian democracy that His Holiness so thoroughly and thoughtfully warned us against in *Veritatis Splendor*. His Holiness wrote:

> Today, when many countries have seen the fall of ideologies which bound politics to a totalitarian conception of the world . . . there is no less grave a danger that the fundamental rights of the human person will be denied and that the religious yearnings which arise in the heart of every human being will be absorbed once again into politics. *This is the risk of an alliance between democracy and ethical relativism,* . . . As history demonstrates, a democracy without values easily turns into open or thinly disguised totalitarianism.

Today, in the midst of a culture war, preserving, or more properly restoring, religious freedom is most important in the area of education. The separation of church and state must not be employed to separate family from education. Schools must enhance, not contradict, the moral formation within family.

Returning to Jefferson's question: Are legs being broken or pockets picked when our tax contributions to the public fund for education are allowed to be directed to religious schools? For the past thirty years or so, this question has left the court in total confusion. There is some obvious coercion in taxation. And because of this the court, with a few not fully explainable exceptions, has denied the direct financial support of private religious schools. But wait a minute, whatever coercion there is in taxation — is coercion in support of education generally, not particular religious belief or practice. Sure, a head tax for the exclusive support of Catholic schools alone would be improper, but a tax yielding funds that are to be generally available to parents for their children's education in public or private schools does not pose this problem.

Here, thankfully, the Supreme Court has started to return to its senses and the original understanding. Aided by the able advocacy of Notre Dame graduate William Bently Ball in a recent decision, the court has opined that "public benefits that are neutrally provided to a broad class of citizens defined without reference to religion" do not implicate an unconstitutional establishment of religion. The court stated that it is an especially easy case when the funds are paid directly to the parents. And so the court has sustained state tax credits that can be used to offset tuition at public or private schools and vocational assistance that can be as freely used for secular avocations as for the study of the ministry.

And in this, there is an important message that concerned Catholic citizens and parents must deliver to every governor of every state, the federal constitution — even as interpreted in 1995 — does *not* preclude the allowance of dollar-for-dollar tuition tax credits or the use of school vouchers at public or private, including private religious, schools. If governors and the legislatures decline to make education funds available to all their citizens who have obediently contributed to this public tax fund, they will need some excuse other than the religion clauses of the First Amendment.

Is there another legal excuse? Regrettably, as the Mount Soledad case suggests, there are often troubling obstacles to religious freedom now lurking in state constitutions as well. For example, Article VIII, section 2, paragraph 2 of the Michigan constitution prohibits "the payment of public monies to support the attendance of any student or the employment of any person at any nonpublic school." How extraordinary this provision is. Think: If tomorrow the state legislature announced that public funding for housing or economic development or research would be available to everyone except those who are inclined to vote for William Bennett for President, we would have little difficulty articulating the words: "they can't do that," and we would be right. Such inequality and selectivity would be the grossest violation of our First Amendment guarantee to free speech and the Fourteenth Amendment's assurance of equal justice under law. If the same public funds for housing, economic development, and research were given to all, save people of faith, we would just as easily see that as unconstitutional religious discrimination.

How then can such state prohibitions of the funding of private schools be justified? If you're thinking that it is necessary to satisfy the constitutional requirement of separation of church and state, you haven't been paying close attention. While such might have been the case twenty or thirty years ago when some of these prohibitions were added to state constitutions, the Supreme Court has made it reasonably clear recently that this is no longer true. If you're thinking that the prohibition can be saved because it does not overtly discriminate against private religious schools, but rather by its terms excludes all nonpublic schools, think again. U.S. Supreme Court precedent finds a violation of the free exercise clause when a state requires that a citizen forego a religious practice in order to be eligible for public benefits. A statute's neutral appearance is insufficient to save it from constitutional scrutiny.

No, not only are any state constitutional prohibitions of funding for private school students not required by the U.S. Constitution, they are arguably contrary to the free exercise of religion guaranteed by it. In addition to the interests of religious freedom, parents have a federal constitutional right to direct the upbringing of their children, subject only to reasonable regulation. As a father of five children, let me be clear: It is *not* reasonable regulation to confiscate a family's educational resources and then insist that they be devoted to educational providers that undermine the family or are antagonistic to the family's religious tradition.

It will take courage for the state legislatures and governors to address this longstanding inequity in school funding. But their federal constitutional responsibilities can best be satisfied by leaving education tax dollars in the hands of parent-taxpayers and allowing them complete freedom to spend this money wisely in the school of their choice — public or private.

This is by my reckoning a governor's duty. It is a legislature's duty. This is not just another policy argument to think about, and none of us should be satisfied with pseudo-performance of this duty, either in the form of vouchers only within public schools or in some manufactured creature called "chartered schools." I have never had it fully explained to me what a "chartered school" is, but I know this, it gives me the same unsettled feeling as "chartered health insurance from a federally-mandated regional health alliance." In both cases, the choice offered will be no choice. In both cases, we will be yielding to government what our Catholic tradition of subsidiarity, and our national tradition of federalism, tell us is more appropriately handled within the family or local community. In both cases, we will be forfeiting the natural law legacy of the American republic.

Tocqueville forewarned us of the consequences of this forfeiture when he wrote:

> Having thus taken each citizen in turn in its powerful grasp and shaped him to its will, government then extends its embrace to include the whole of society. It covers the whole of social life with a network of petty, complicated rules that are both minute and uniform, through which even men of the greatest originality and the most vigorous temperament cannot force their heads above the crowd. It does not break men's will, but softens, bends, . . . hinders, restrains, enervates, stifles, and stultifies so much that in the end each nation is no more than a flock of timid and hardworking animals with the government as its shepherd.

This was not the America or the Americans Tocqueville saw in 1830. What he found were Americans independent and free and informed by personal reliance in public and private upon unashamed biblical teaching and religion. He found a young nation with a moral and social order derived from the transcendent value of the human person created in God's image.

What would he find today?

Let us be tenacious and resolute in our desire to sustain our faith, and with it, the central pillar of genuine religious freedom, upon which the American Republic stands.

Catholic Conscience and the Law

William Gladstone's *Expostulation* attacking the dogma of papal infallibility for allegedly reducing Catholic citizens to a condition of mental and moral slavery elicited a letter of congratulation from Otto von Bismarck. The German Reich Chancellor expressed to the former English Prime Minister his "deep and hopeful gratification to see the two nations, which in Europe are the champions of the liberty of conscience encountering the same foe, [standing] shoulder to shoulder in defending the highest interests of the human race."

Gladstone's attack on papal authority provoked an altogether different reaction from John Henry Newman, who in his *Letter to the Duke of Norfolk* responded to the charge of mental and moral slavery by arguing that recognition of papal authority by Catholic citizens is perfectly consistent with their maintaining freedom of conscience properly understood. Central to Newman's argument was his attack on "the various false senses, philosophical or popular, which in this day are put upon the word 'conscience.' "

> Conscience has rights [Newman argued] because it has duties; but in this age, with a large portion of the public, it is the very right and freedom of conscience to dispense with conscience. . . . Conscience is a stern monitor, but in this century it has been superseded by a counterfeit, which the eighteen centuries prior to it never heard of, and could not have mistaken for it, if they had. It is the right of self-will.

The degenerate senses of "conscience" and "freedom of conscience," whose origins Newman located in the moral and political thought of the nineteenth century, have become deeply entrenched in our culture. Consider how common it is for people to reason as follows: "My conscience does not tell me that X is wrong; therefore X is not wrong for me." Or, even more egregiously: "My conscience does not tell me that X is wrong (wrong for me); therefore I have a right to do X as a matter of freedom of conscience." Every manner of evil and injustice is today rationalized, defended, and insulated from rebuke by appeal to conscience.

The corrupt conception of conscience implicit in these appeals has even come to occupy a pivotal place in American constitutional jurisprudence. Last year, a federal district judge struck down Washington state's prohibition of physician-assisted suicide, citing as authority the decision of the Supreme Court of the United States in the 1992 case of *Planned Parenthood vs. Casey.* The judge quoted a now famous sentence from the plurality opinion of Justices O'Connor, Kennedy, and Souter which Notre Dame Law Professor Gerard V. Bradley has labeled "the mystery passage" in which the justices announce their discovery of what Professor Bradley calls "the mega-right":

> At the heart of liberty [the justices declare] is the right to define one's own concepts of existence, of meaning, of the universe, and of the mystery of human life.

Although the word "conscience" does not appear in the mystery passage, we should have no difficulty perceiving in the justices' conception of "liberty" the idea of "self-will" which Newman condemned as the counterfeit of conscience.

Conscience vs. Self-Will

Conscience, authentically understood, is the very opposite of defining for oneself the meaning of life or manufacturing one's own moral universe. It is, rather, nothing less than reason's last, best judgment specifying the bearing of moral principles one knows, yet in no way makes up for oneself, on concrete proposals for action. In thus identifying one's specific *duties* under the moral law, conscience is indeed "a stern monitor."

Contrast this understanding of conscience with its counterfeit. Conscience as what Newman called "self-will" is a matter of emotion, not reason. It is concerned not with the identification of what one has a duty to do or not to do, one's feelings to the contrary notwithstanding, but rather, and precisely, with sorting out one's feelings. Conscience as "self-will" identifies permissions, not obligations. It licenses behavior by establishing that one doesn't feel bad about doing it, or, at least, doesn't feel so bad about doing it that one prefers the alternative of not doing it.

At a time when famous Catholic public officials, supported, in some cases, by prominent Catholic theologians, appeal to "respect for conscience" in justifying — or rather, let us not mince words, in rationalizing — their advocacy of legal abortion, damaging and ultimately deadly embryo experimentation, and even the public funding of these atrocities, we would do well to recall the teaching of *Gaudium et Spes*, the "Pastoral Constitution on the

Church in the Modern World" of the Second Vatican Council:

> In the depths of his conscience, man detects a law which he does not impose upon himself, but which holds him to obedience. Always summoning him to love good and avoid evil, the voice of conscience can when necessary speak to his heart more specifically: do this, shun that. For man has in his heart a law written by God. To obey it is the very dignity of man; according to it he will be judged. (#16)

And here the Fathers of the Council cite the verses in St. Paul's Letter to the Romans which speak of a law known even to the Gentiles, who have not the law of Moses, because it is written on the hearts of all men — the "natural law" which, though illumined by God's revelation, is accessible even to unaided reason.

It is this law which binds in conscience all of us — Catholics, Protestants, Jews, members of every community of faith and even those without faith — not simply to refrain from taking innocent human life but to avoid the injustice of supporting policies which deprive the unborn and elderly of the protection against wrongful killing to which every member of the human family is strictly entitled. The moral prohibitions of abortion and euthanasia are examples of the "negative" norms of the natural law which apply, as Pope John Paul II recently reminded us in the encyclical *Veritatis Splendor*, always and everywhere to everyone alike.

But, of course, the requirements of morality are not exhausted by these negative norms. The vast majority of our moral duties are affirmative, not negative — norms such as "feed the hungry," "stand with victims of injustice," "foster the common good." These precepts are no less, and no less integral, parts of the natural law than are the negative norms; nor is it the case that our obligations under the affirmative norms are any less stringent. Conscience, properly informed, requires more — much more — than the mere avoidance of the sort of wrongdoing involved in, say, having an abortion, or performing or paying for abortions, or supporting legal abortion and its public funding. All of us, whether we recognize it or not, are morally bound affirmatively to combat injustice and other evils, and not merely to avoid unjustly inflicting evil on others.

However, affirmative norms differ from negative ones in an important respect. There is no single, uniquely correct way of fulfilling affirmative responsibilities. The precise nature of such responsibilities, in fact, varies in significant ways from person to person, depending on people's circumstances, commitments, and opportunities, not to mention their talents and abilities.

Legitimate Relativity

The problem of unjust laws usefully illustrates the difference between negative and affirmative obligations. Consider a law requiring Catholic physicians or hospitals to perform, or, at least, refer for abortions. Now, what this law would demand is strictly excluded by a negative norm; no Catholic physician or hospital could, in conscience, perform or refer for an abortion. The norm applies to everyone and applies to everyone in the same way. The only way to fulfill its requirements is by refusing to comply with the law.

Now, let us consider a different sort of unjust law, the one we already have, namely, a national policy which, while requiring no one to perform or participate in abortions (though the public funding of abortion by certain states requires people to materially cooperate in abortions in ways that, at least, raise a question), fails to protect the right to life of unborn children and severely restricts pro-life efforts to dissuade women from aborting them. The norms to which conscience adverts here are the closely related affirmative obligations to stand with the victims of injustice and to foster the common good. To fulfill our obligations under these norms, we must combat the injustice of legal abortion and abortion funding and work for laws which respect the profound and equal worth and dignity of women and their unborn children. But these affirmative obligations, unlike negative ones, can be fulfilled by different people in different ways. Everyone has an obligation to support the pro-life cause, and to pray for its success, but depending on people's circumstances, commitments, opportunities, talents, and abilities, different people can legitimately support the cause in different ways and with different levels of involvement.

No one should conclude from this legitimate relativity, however, that his or her own responsibilities in the face of the grave injustice of our abortion laws is a matter of moral indifference. Our duties under the relevant affirmative norms are relative to our individual circumstances, but, given my circumstances or your circumstances, you or I may be strictly bound in conscience to make a particular, and possibly quite substantial, contribution to the cause of justice for the unborn. Our duties in conscience, though particular to each of us as individuals, may be no more optional in this case, than in the case of negative norms. Even when it comes to affirmative norms, conscience is a stern monitor.

Moreover, as Catholic Christians, who must discern the requirements of conscience in light of the Gospel, each of us must consider that he or she is called by Christ himself to do more than merely meet the moral minimum of the natural law. One way or another, the Lord calls each of us to self-sacrificing love. Recall the story from the tenth chapter of St. Mark's gospel:

> . . . a man ran up and knelt before [Jesus], and asked him, "Good Teacher, what must I do to inherit eternal life?" And Jesus said to him, ". . . You know the commandments: 'Do not kill, Do not commit adultery, Do not steal, Do not bear false witness, Do not defraud, Honor your father and mother.' " [The young man replied], "Teacher, all these I have observed from my youth." And Jesus looking upon him loved him, "You lack one thing; go, sell what you have, and give to the poor, and you will have treasure in heaven; and come, follow me." At that saying his countenance fell, and he went away sorrowful for he had great possessions.

More Than a Moral Minimum

The story of the rich young man reveals just how stern a monitor Christian conscience can be. Although, the challenge for the young man was to sacrifice his riches for the gospel, for each of us it may be something else. Perhaps in the cause of justice for the unborn (or some other just cause) we are called by Christ to risk reputation, so-called social respectability, prospects for career advancement, friends or family, health or comfort. Each of us must pray and reflect upon our own unique circumstances, opportunities, talents, and abilities in making the judgment of conscience required of us in the matter.

It is in "the depths of conscience" that we discern the specific content of Christ's call to each of us to "go and sell what you have, then come and follow me." For no two of us are the implications of Christ's call precisely the same. So each of us must discern these implications for himself. For some, Christ's call is to a life of secluded contemplation; for others it is a call to dramatic, even heroic, public witness.

In no one's case, however, is it easy to accept Christ's call, for each of us, in his own way, has "many possessions." Even the upright among us will be tempted to say, "But I have kept the commandments; I have met the obligations of the moral law, both negative and affirmative; is that not enough?" The Gospel's answer is "No, that is not enough." There is one thing more; and that one thing takes us beyond the law to the imitation of Christ's own sacrificial love. Let no one who hears our Lord's call forget, however, that God does not fail to provide the grace each of us needs to follow Christ, wherever he leads — even to the cross. Recall that after the rich young man "went away sorrowful," Jesus horrified His disciples by remarking, "It is easier for a camel to go through the eye of a needle than for a rich man to enter the kingdom of God." "Then who," the disciples asked, "can be saved?" "With men," Jesus replied, "it is impossible, but not with God; for all things are possible with God."

With faith, then, that God will provide, let us, each in his own way — having discerned his obligations in conscience in light of his own unique circumstances, opportunities, and talents — go and sell what he has, and then come and follow Christ. Of none of us let it be said that, upon hearing the Lord's call, he went away sorrowful, for he had many possessions.

Integrating the Faith Into a Corporate Environment

From the beginning of my business career, I was determined to put my faith into practice — to integrate my faith into this corporate environment I was entering. Though I may have wanted such efforts to remain exclusively in my business life, through the influence of everything from Polish nuns, C. S. Lewis, and the rosary to baseball, football coaches, and an occasional lawsuit, this integration of faith found its way into my personal life as well.

Priorities to Live By

I was born on the feast of the annunciation in 1937 to a very poor family. My father died on Christmas eve in 1941 when I was four years old and I was brought up primarily in a Catholic orphanage by very devout Polish nuns. That's where I received my faith, for which I'm forever grateful. I spent most of my junior-high and high school years working on farms (except for a time in the seminary from which I was expelled because they told me I didn't have a vocation). After high school I joined the Marine corps.

While I was in the Marine corps I was aboard ship, and I had about two weeks on the ocean. One thing I was good at was day dreaming. I was probably world class. I was laying on my bunk thinking what I was going to do when I got out of the Marines, all the successes I was going to have, the kind of life-style I was going to live, and you can bet it was the ultimate. But then I had this feeling, an emptiness that led me to ask myself, "So what? Is that going to make me happy?" Out of that time came, I think, some of the most profound thinking I've ever done in my life, before or since, and that was when I came up with my five priorities for life.

Those five priorities are spiritual, social, mental, physical, and financial — in that order.

Spiritual. I was smart enough to know that no matter what I gained, if I lost my soul, I wouldn't have gained anything. So, even though I knew the financial was very important to me, I didn't put it first among my priorities.

Social. It was also important to me that I have a strong family life so social was important. I wanted to be a good father, a good husband, and practice the golden rule.

Mental. I knew that most people use only ten percent of their brains. I wanted to be using more of mine than that. I wanted it to wear out, not rust out.

Physical. Physical health was also more important than my pocket book — I realized that if I lost my health I would give every penny I could to get it back, so that had to be more important than my pocket book.

Financial. So, that gave me license, as long as I didn't violate those other four higher priorities, to go out and make all the money I wanted. That was basically my road map for life. I didn't think money was bad. I thought of money in the hands of good people — money buys Bibles, money pays for seminary education, and so on.

Integrating Priorities in Business

The question most often asked is what's a guy with a name like Monaghan doing in the pizza business? I was in school at the University of Michigan, but I didn't have the money to stay in school. My brother knew about this pizza place that was available nearby for a $500 down payment. I had no idea what the total price was and I still don't to this day. It was the most humble beginning you could imagine.

We managed to borrow the money for the down payment. I thought this was going to pay my way through college. I ended up working nearly one hundred hours a week and losing money — that's not a good way to get through college. After six months, my brother decided he wanted out of the business so I bought his half-interest for a Volkswagen delivery car. It's been a rocky road, but right from the beginning I realized I was stuck in the pizza business: I wasn't going to get back in college, I was in my mid-twenties at this time, and still a freshmen. And, I didn't want to give up something that I had started.

I was determined to be successful. I wanted to show the world that you can be successful in business without being dishonest. In my circle, at that time, it was believed that if you were successful, you either married it, inherited it, or you stole it. I didn't believe that, I believed the opposite; in fact, I still do.

So, I needed some way to make this pizza business work. I came up with the concept of delivery as a specialty. There were pizza places that delivered before I came along, but they delivered because they had to, not because they wanted to. I was the first one that delivered because I wanted to. So I got rid of everything else that was on the menu, got rid of the tables, and streamlined the operation so I could concentrate on delivery because delivery is tough. Everybody wants to pick up the phone at lunch so that concept led me to spurts of success. I'd get successful, then I'd get into a bad partnership. Then I had a fire and no insurance to cover my loss. Then I over-expanded and lost control of the business, getting it back after the franchisees got angry and sued the company.

I spent a couple of years working seven days a week, surviving day to day. Finally, just as I was beginning to feel some success, a few bad officers in the company went to the creditors to try to get the company from me. And then I was hit with a law suit from Domino sugar — a billion dollar company against me, a struggling regional chain. Five years of litigation and we lost. On appeal we won. Domino sugar took it to the Supreme Court which refused to hear the case. Five years, it sapped us of what little assets we had in the company.

Then in 1980 we took off like a rocket. We had about 350 stores in 1980. By 1990 we had about 5,300 stores. And we were the fastest-growing restaurant chain in the history of the restaurant industry. In 1985, we opened 954 stores, the most units opened by any restaurant chain in history.

We did it the hard way, no additional franchise fees, no outsiders that bought franchises. I built the company by that time into one that boasted 2.5 billion dollars in sales. We're number one in the pizza industry with some fifty-four percent of all the pizzas delivered in the United States. We're number two in the pizza business (actually there was one quarter in which we passed Pizza Hut as the number one pizza seller in the United States). At one time, we were the seventh largest restaurant chain in the world, and we've won all kinds of awards. I believe we are estimated to be worth a billion dollars according to *Fortune.*

I got into other businesses, mostly turnarounds, and they were lots of fun because Domino's was working like clock work. That's the business side of it.

Integrating Priorities at Home

I think I realized I wanted to be a billionaire saint. I figured if St. Louis can be a king and be a saint, then I can too. I felt that they were compatible. I still do. In fact, I think they can be complimentary. My justification for being successful and not hiding it was simply this: money gets people's attention; people listen to money.

I felt that if I was visibly successful, then I'd be a better witness because more people would see my example. On the other hand, I had this materialistic side. The first ostentatious thing I did was buy the Detroit Tigers, my lifelong dream. It was the biggest sports story in the state of Michigan in over ten years. It was front page for three days solid in the Detroit media. And of course the following year we went out and won the World Series: We were 35 and 5 at the beginning of the season and we went on to win the World Series. It was quite a high for a guy who was brought up in an orphanage. In 1989 we sponsored an Indy Car. We won the Indy 500. So, I might be one of the few if not the only person in the world to win the World Series and the Indy 500.

I built a gigantic building for our corporate headquarters, world class — architecture's been a hobby of mine my entire life. I got into airplanes, helicopters, yachts, an incredible lodge in northern Michigan on Drummond island. I built a championship golf course. I had one of the finest car collections in the country. I put together one of the greatest art collections and was ranked as one of the top 100 collectors in the country. I became somewhat of an expert on what was the best of everything.

I think I knew more about what the best of everything was than most people, even the best tailors. I even know what the best cigars are and I don't smoke. To me, it was important to know what the best was and go after it.

I stayed at the best hotels in the world. I vacationed at the best places, ate at the best restaurants. But the big thing was my house. Here's a guy who all his life was a frustrated architect (as well as a frustrated priest). I finally was building the house of my dreams and this was going to be the house of houses. I hired the greatest architect in the world, planned this thing for years, got the right sight, right environment, and started building the house. I stopped a third of the way through, after spending about seven million dollars.

I felt pretty guilty about that house. Everything else I did, no matter how expensive it was or how luxurious, I had justification — business justification. But with the house, I didn't quite have that. I felt pretty guilty about it. I talked to a priest about it and he said "oh, it's your own money; you earned it; no reason why you can't spend it." That wasn't good enough. Still, I felt guilty. But, I'm getting ahead of myself. Anyway, I started building this fantastic house. . . . Meanwhile, my spiritual side was busy, too.

Spirituality

I was trying to improve myself and one of the things that helped was that in 1974 I read that professional football coach, Don Shula, one of my heroes, went to Mass every day. So, I figured, if he can go to Mass every day, I can go to Mass every day. During one of those Masses in 1974, the priest gave a homily about the rosary. He said every time Mary appeared, she urged people to say the rosary. I thought, if Mary wants to say the rosary that bad, the least I could do is say the rosary every day. And it's ironic because, at that very same time, I began to be successful in business. It took that long; I'm sure there's a connection.

Soon after this, they changed the time of the daily Mass at my parish, making it difficult for me to attend. The result was my asking the bishop if I could celebrate Mass at the office. He gave his approval as long as we didn't use a parish priest and we didn't take up a collection (there was one more stipulation but I can't remember what it was). And so, we've had daily Mass at the office ever since. We have a corporate chapel. We have a priest in the area who regularly says Mass and also a lot of priests who say Mass while they are visiting the area. And we've been doing that now for about fourteen years. I don't know why more people don't do it. To me, it's the greatest perk you can give your employees. What perk can be better than giving them access to a chapel?

I started a foundation in the early 1980's. One of the conclusions I came to for this foundation was that I wasn't going to cure people from cancer because they might end up going to hell anyhow, even if their physical lives were saved! So I was going to spend my money trying to get people to go to heaven. I figured with the limited amount of dollars I had, I wanted to get as many people to heaven as possible. That was the criteria for our foundation.

I also got involved in missions in Honduras quite accidentally. It has been very rewarding for me.

After I met the Pope for the first time in 1987, I started Legatus, an organization for Catholic CEO's. They have chapters all over the country.

My next adventure started because of the tendency of the courts a few years ago of ruling against the presence of creches in public buildings. It upset me so I decided on the grounds of this great big new building I had, right on the expressway with 80,000 cars a day going by, that I was going to put up the largest Christmas light display they'd ever seen. And it was going to be spiritual — no Santa Clauses, no Rudolphs, or anything like that. We had 400,000 people going by so you can imagine we did have a few traffic jams. The next year I was going to do it and the township decided I couldn't. So we went to court. We spent $110,000 and won. The idea is to keep Christ in Christmas. In 1994 we had a display of over two hundred creches.

Another thing I started doing on my spiritual side is reading more, reading a lot about apologetics, reading about my faith. Also, I try to share my faith publicly. I have interviews with some media. Wherever I can, I try to be a witness. If they ask what my daily routine is, I tell them I start out by saying three rosaries, then I run, then I go to Mass. If they ask me if I go to Mass every day I say yes.

One day I had an interview with the *Chicago Tribune*, with the religious editor. Sometimes I get a little devil in me, and it was so this particular day. The editor was talking to me about why Catholics don't do this or they don't do that, they don't believe this or that. I replied, "Not all Catholics understand their faith. In fact the best Catholics are converts because they really have to think their way into the Church." Then I went on to say — and I knew I'd get into trouble, but I couldn't stop myself — "I can't understand why any thinking Christian doesn't become Catholic." That's one of the few times they printed what I said verbatim. Did I get the hate mail and the hate calls! But I tell you, it just told me I hit a nerve and I'm sure it didn't do any harm; it might have done some good somewhere.

Courage and Conviction

The National Organization of Women (NOW) wanted to do a fund-raiser at Domino's Farms. When I heard about it, I said no and they sued us. We won. Then the Attorney General sued us again and we won, after hundreds and thousands of dollars in legal fees.

During the 1980's in the state of Michigan, there was a referendum on the ballot to stop tax-funded abortions. It wasn't looking good for our side and someone asked me if I would give $50,000 and go on television making a pitch for the referendum. I did. I knew I was sticking my neck out a little bit; I had no idea how much I was sticking my neck out, and the roof caved in.

NOW got on this one like you wouldn't believe, *Ms.* magazine and everything else of that ilk got all over me, even pornographic magazines got on me. The franchisees started getting letters from the NOW organization. They did a national boycott against

Domino's Pizza all over the nation and I thought, "Oh my gosh, what can I do about this?" It was a terribly helpless feeling: What could I do about it, how could I stop it?

Then somewhere along the line I got the greatest feeling I ever had in my life. And it must be the kind of feeling that martyrs get; there's some kind of grace that must come to them and enable them to go on. I could see why martyrs die with smiles on their faces. I came to the conclusion that if my life's work goes down the tube, at least it's for a good cause. And the truth of the matter is, it did nothing but help us.

There are some franchisees that are pro-choice that I can't convince otherwise, but my mail was twenty-six to one in favor of the pro-life position. We may have lost ten percent of our customers because of my pro-life stand, but we picked up that many or more that we didn't have before. We were on network television. As a cardinal told me then, "Tom, there's no such thing as bad publicity." Well, I think it helped.

Freedom

In my Catholic reading I came across a book, *Mere Christianity*, by C. S. Lewis. In this book, Lewis writes about sin, specifically the sin of pride. Pride is the greatest of sins; I knew that from catechism. Lewis's words hit me right between the eyes. I had been in the process of building this house, deciding whether I should go ahead or not go ahead, and my whole life passed before me. I saw myself as a kid, how I was more competitive than other kids on the playing field. I saw myself in business, working harder to get what I wanted than other people would, more ambitious than other people. I saw myself as always wanting the best. Lewis's words told me what I really was: I was the most pride-filled person I knew, and if pride was the greatest of all sins, what did that make me?

I felt pretty humble after that. From that moment on, I decided to take what I called a millionaire's vow of poverty. I was married so I couldn't become a monk, but I did decide I was going to give up luxuries for life. I wasn't going to drive a luxury car any more, I wasn't going to own any more boats or airplanes. I wasn't going to fly first-class. I've been faithful to that vow for over three years now, and I wait in line at airports. I no longer have a chauffeur.

What a sense of freedom it is to give up those things.

When I was having problems with the NOW boycott and I realized that my actions have impact on other people's lives, I decided maybe I should sell the company and devote myself full time to my Catholic projects and my foundation. So, in 1989 I decided to sell the company. I picked the worst time in history to sell a company. The banks were having problems of their own. There wasn't money to finance something like this. Milken had just gone to jail, junk bonds disappeared on Wall Street, insurance companies were having problems, the S & L's were having problems.

Meanwhile, instead of focusing on running the company, we focused on selling the company. This went on for two years. We couldn't find a buyer that would pay any where near what the company was worth. So my only choice, I realized, was that I had to come back and put the company back together. Maybe that's where God wanted me after all. Maybe I can be a better witness running a company than running a foundation.

I came back with a strategy based on that of Vince

Lombardi. He asked his players to consider making three things priorities: God, family, and the Packers. So I substituted Domino's for the Packers. I thought I could turn this thing around in three months, because I had turned the company around many times before. The situation was a lot worse than I thought it was. I mean it was really bad. The franchisees were in an upheaval, sales and profits had all but disappeared, the media was attacking us, the Tigers were starting to lose money, bank defaults all over the place, corporate and personal. I had a great big building — 300,000 square feet of empty space. Yes, 1992 was a terrible year.

We sold the Tigers to our competitors. A lot of people said that was stupid. It was the smartest thing I ever did because our sales were up and theirs were down. And you know where baseball ended up in 1994. We closed about 500 stores and laid off about 600 staff. We sold all the non-pizza business, the radio stations, television stations, hotels, shopping centers, computer companies, my cars, my Frank Lloyd Wright collection. (You know, collections are fun but they're totally selfish and useless, I found. They don't do anything for society. It's okay to collect stamps or something, but when you get into millions of dollars, it's prideful is what it is).

The second year, 1994, we had a record profit, the most profit we had ever had in our company, and the debt was the lowest it's ever been in ten or twelve years.

Not too many people get a second chance like this. I feel fortunate. Experience has taught me a great deal about integrating faith in business. I'm going to make sure this time it's for the glory of God.

The Emerging Catholic Voice:
Integrating the Mystical Body of Christ Into
the Mainstream of American Life

In my attempts to address the emerging Catholic voice in America, I must admit to having felt a special kinship with the "Little Drummer Boy." Nothing I wrote seemed "good enough"; no words seemed to capture the joyful anticipation that had been in my heart when I first accepted this invitation to be a part of the Catholic Campaign's first Leadership Conference.

It was in taking a quiet moment to pray away this paralyzing sense of inadequacy that a simple discovery bordering on insight began to take shape. I recalled a recent journal entry where I had scribbled in three a.m. handwriting, "At the root of any inability to give of oneself openly is always a crisis of faith, hope or love; sometimes, all three."

Faith, Hope, and Love

My still blank writing tablet was a solid reminder to work on all three of these virtues in preparation for this writing:

1) to fortify my own faith in the true source of all inspiration;
2) to intensify my own hope in the limitless potential for good to emerge whenever "two or more are gathered in His Name" (Mt 18:20); and,
3) to deepen my own love for each fellow pilgrim who

has responded to His call "by name" in choosing to read these words.

I am grateful for the opportunity to explore the "ten principles of public Catholicism" (see pp. 16-17) which so eloquently express the "emerging Catholic Voice." I believe we have become a voice crying in the wilderness (cf. Mt 3:3) . . . in the darkened wasteland we now call the "mainstream of American life."

So many voices . . . a contemporary tower of Babel made up of educated and simple, rich and poor, male and female, young and old. At times we may even convince ourselves that we, the laity, no longer have anything meaningful left in common. In our more honest moments we must glance in horror into the spiritual mirror and see reflected a collective face scarred by fear, despair, and apathy. Whatever happened to the face we once knew radiating faith, hope, and love?

Can this discordant chorus of too many self-anointed soloists once again become a harmonizing choir of finely-tuned parts? Is there still room for "love" to slip in between the pronouns of "me, myself, and I"? Can faith be restored to the living, breathing invitation to grace that it once was before our indifference and despair choked its lifeline? Can hope still find a place at the table alongside faith and love so that our passion for life can once again be heard between the lines of every "choice" we make?

I believe that the answer to all of these questions is a resounding "yes," *provided* we take seriously the twin calls to conscience and to action that are deeply embedded within the "ten principles of public Catholicism."

On a lighter note, you might ask how could any

Catholic *not* take seriously a list of "commands" configured as "ten"? Even as I smile at this historical analogy, I find it sobering to admit how challenging it has been for most of us to follow the laws of God — let alone ten principles authored by the Catholic Campaign for America! And so, let's set about our task at hand with humility and renewed determination recognizing that our mission is at once significant and formidable.

The greatest Teacher of all time taught us through His parables the importance of using symbols and colorful analogies when trying to communicate the meaning and importance of a difficult message. We recall, for example, that when He addressed a gathering of shepherds, He would refer to Himself as the "Lamb of God." When He spoke to farmers or laborers in the fields, He would adapt His self-portrait to the "Vine and the branches." When dining with His friends, He would describe Himself as the "Bread of Life." These powerful images enabled His audience to immediately visualize what He was trying to convey.

The Mystical Body

I believe that if our Lord were speaking with us tonight, He would hear our need as a lay faith community for an enlightening symbol and would perhaps draw upon the "Mystical Body" to penetrate our confusion. He would then find an effective way to weave the ten principles of public Catholicism into this powerful symbol which could be integrated into the needy mainstream of American life.

I recall as a child being particularly moved by this image of Christ's Mystical Body. This symbol stood apart from all others in its ability to vividly convey the intimate bond that exists among the laity, the Church and Christ. Recognizing this relationship, the passage in Paul to the Corinthians takes on deeper significance, "If one member suffers, all suffer together; if one member is honored, all rejoice together." (1 Cor 12:26)

The interdependence, mutual support, and unity suggested by this living symbol of Christ's Mystical Body are precisely the qualities that are needed among the laity at this time in our Church's history. They are also the very qualities being requested of us in the ten principles of public Catholicism. Unless we resolve to abide by these principles, the Mystical Body as we are forming it today will remain injured, anemic, and fractured almost beyond recognition.

More often than not, one hand literally does not know what the other hand is doing. And when it does, it is usually hard at work criticizing, second-guessing, and condemning the work of others. The Head of our Mystical Body must feel at once torn apart by the divisiveness of some of our members and fatigued by the apathy and indifference that distinguish the rest.

How can this Mystical Body of which we are an integral part be made healthy and whole again? How can "one Bread, one Body" once again mean more than just the lyrics to a pretty song? The answer rests in our ability to embrace the ten principles. These principles could be thought of as the medicine or "wonder drug" for our weakened Mystical Body.

The Ten Principles Reordered

When challenged to understand any list of behavioral principles or codes of conduct, it is often helpful to look for natural groupings of thought or categories of ideas. In applying this learning device to our list of ten principles of public Catholicism, I discovered an interesting grammatical fact. Our list is actually comprised of an unusual mix of suggestions presented as verbs, adjectives, and adverbs. While this realization might delight my high school English teacher, it is hardly worthy of your attention unless I can demonstrate that it relates directly to our ability to understand and to implement the principles at hand.

In reordering these ten principles according to their grammatical categories, the list takes on much richer meaning. We can now identify, for example, three verb-based principles that are our "calls to action" and seven adverb and adjective-based principles that are our "calls to conscience." We can hear a new coherence and implicit priority among our ten principles as we discern those that suggest "what" we should do and those that tell us "how" to do it.

For example, to suggest that we, the laity, should "*engage* the present culture with the liberating power of faith" is quite different than asking that we do so "*humbly*." Similarly, to suggest that the laity should "*consistently integrate* our faith into every aspect of our lives" is not the same kind of request as asking us to do so "*charitably*."

Three Calls to Action

To be specific, the three principles that represent "calls to action" are those that request the laity to:
1) "*become knowledgeable* in our faith";
2) "*consistently integrate* our faith into every aspect of our lives"; and,

3) *actively "engage* the present culture with the
liberating power of our faith."

Seven Calls to Conscience

The remaining seven principles will make it
possible for us to carry out these three "calls to action."
These prerequisites are our "calls to conscience." They
lay the groundwork and offer the grace-filled
perspective that will make an effective lay witness
possible. They can be meaningfully divided into two
groups:

1) the three that offer the essential character traits
that we must develop; and,

2) the four that tell us in what Christ-like manner we
are to perform our tasks.

Three Character Traits. In order to put our
action-based tenets into practice, we must be willing to
develop certain fundamental character traits. They are
courage, responsibility, and loyalty. Without these in
place, it is unlikely that we will ever be able to make
our witness meaningful and effective. For example,
unless we can develop within ourselves the qualities of
courage, personal *responsibility*, and *loyalty*, how can
we expect to "consistently integrate our faith into every
aspect of our lives."

Four Christ-like Qualities. The remaining four
principles are also "calls to conscience," but in a
different way. We must be willing to develop within
ourselves four Christ-like qualities: *humility*, *charity*,
pride, and *optimism*. In fact, I would go so far as to say
that the only way that we will be able to successfully
accomplish our three calls to action is if we can learn to

manifest these qualities in our relationship with God and neighbor.

Whenever I want to put an idea to the ultimate test, I have found that my toughest critics are our seven- and nine-year old children, Billy and Mary Alana. If their eyes glaze over halfway through my presentation, it is safe to assume that the concept is probably too complex or esoteric to be of much merit to a public audience; if they yawn midstream through my explanation, it's a high probability that the so-called insight is so obvious as to warrant a response like, "Next?"

The good news is that neither child "glazed over" or yawned, but they did pose an interesting challenge to test the validity of our proposed reorganization of principles. I was asked if I could combine all ten into one meaningful (albeit pretty long!) sentence that would put each to work in the grammatical form that would make the most sense.

Well, let's give it a try: "We, the laity, must develop certain character traits — *courage*, personal *responsibility*, and *loyalty* — in order to perform certain required tasks — *become knowledgeable* in our faith, *consistently integrate* this faith into our lives, and *actively engage* the present culture — and we must carry out these actions in a manner consistent with Christ's example — namely, with *humility*, *charity*, *optimism*, and legitimate *pride*."

Three Calls to Conscience:
Courage, Responsibility, and Loyalty

Now that we have successfully reorganized our ten principles, let us consider in greater depth their real meaning for us as individuals and the Church as a whole. In reflecting upon the spiritual stumbling blocks that may have prevented us from living up to these standards, three significant obstacles come to mind.

As a philosophy and logic major in college, I recall being awestruck by a particular Christian existentialist named Gabriel Marcel who wrote in his two-volume treatise entitled *The Mystery of Being* that "all sin is rooted in *fear*, *vanity*, and *desire*." His diagnosis about evil rang true twenty-five years ago and it still does today.

Consider the striking, almost symmetrical contrast between the Catholic Campaign's call for "courage, personal responsibility and loyalty" and Marcel's warning about "fear, vanity and desire." *Courage* and *fear* stand in stark contrast to one another while *responsibility* and *vanity* oppose each other with almost the same antagonistic tension as do *loyalty* and *desire*.

Loyalty vs. Desire

How many times have we sacrificed our loyalty to the Church, the Holy Father, or the Magisterium on the altar of our desire to be "politically correct"? How many times have we compromised our faithfulness to the teachings of the Church because of a desire to be accepted or promoted or included as part of the so-called "mainstream"?

Gabriel Marcel was right. "Desire" is a sneaky demon that creeps in unannounced — making us laugh at inappropriate Catholic jokes and overlook our denial of Him far more than just three times. Without a renewal of loyalty, every tenet of our faith will soon be up for grabs; every teaching of our Church will have to withstand a popularity contest.

Personal Responsibility vs. Vanity

What can Marcel's sin of vanity tell us about the principle of personal responsibility? How can we be "sensitive to the appropriate role of the hierarchy" when we see our role magnified out of any reasonable proportion through the distorted lens of vanity? When the laity's concerns are centered around diocesan titles, staff size, and program budgets, we can be sure that vanity has taken front and center.

On the other end of the spectrum, it has become convenient to blame the hierarchy for the laity's weakened sense of responsibility claiming that our voice hasn't been requested or heard. My own experience tells me something quite different. Too often the laity have seen the Church as a convenient vehicle in which to reenact their unresolved power struggles. Why shouldn't the clergy think twice before opening a Pandora's box filled with shrill demands for "women's rights" and unreasonable applications of a much-abused word called "choice"? When vanity punctuates any discussion, all of the sentences end in exclamation points. There are no humble question marks and no conciliatory periods.

On a more remedial note, social scientists have identified three conditions that are necessary in order for a person to feel a strong sense of personal responsibility. First, a person must feel *uniquely qualified* to perform the task at hand; second, the individual must believe that the task is *do-able*; and third, the individual must feel a sense of *importance* and even *urgency* about the need to perform the task.

With the spiritual block of vanity set aside, I must say that the laity has every reason to feel an enhanced sense of responsibility and opportunity at this time in our Church's history. Perhaps never before has the need been so great or so urgent for a lay renewal, the authentic kind that could be born out of this inspired gathering. This could, indeed, be "the Catholic moment" in the history of our nation provided we have the good sense to draw on each other as resources and speak out energetically.

Courage vs. Fear

Let's take a moment now to examine our third and final character-based principle and consider how we are doing in the timeless war between courage and fear. How can we manifest anything close to courage when we no longer consider rhetorical the biblical question, "If God is for us, who can be against us?" (cf. Rom 8:31)

With the undermining of our faith has come a weakening in our resolve to stand up to the attacks that come incessantly from every form of the media. Courage is not about feeling the absence of fear — but about summoning the strength to overcome that fear for a higher good. If the laity can no longer discern a higher good or, perhaps worse, lack any hope that their voice can make a difference, why are we surprised to see fear elbow out courage in the public arena where opinion polls replace moral absolutes?

I believe that Marcel had his finger on the pulse of America's laity when he warned against fear, vanity, and desire as the moral equivalents to terminal cancer. We need an immediate and massive dose of the antidotes of courage, responsibility, and loyalty. These are the prerequisites to being able to accomplish the three "calls to action" of the Catholic Campaign.

For without *"personal responsibility"* we will not feel compelled to *"become knowledgeable* in our faith"; without *"loyalty,"* we will lack the fortitude to *"consistently integrate* our faith into every dimension of our lives"; and without *"courage,"* we will lack the ardor to *"actively engage* the present culture with the liberating power of our faith."

Four Principles of Manner:
Humility, Charity, Pride, and Optimism

Let's now turn our attention to the four principles that highlight the manner in which we should carry out our role as the laity. Specifically, we are called upon to act with *"humility," "charity,"* legitimate *"pride," and "optimism."*

As I reflected upon why we are failing to live up to these principles, another page of my spiritual history came back into focus. It's not a page that I'm proud of, but it is one that could be instructive for us today.

I recalled the time in my own life when practicing these principles had posed the greatest difficulty. It seemed reasonable to assume that if I could distill the similarities between the circumstances then and now, perhaps I could begin to isolate the root causes preventing the laity as a whole from being more humble, charitable, optimistic, and proud of their Church and their faith.

The lens of my memory "zoomed-in" with

unforgiving accuracy on my less-than-inspired years as a graduate student at Harvard Business School. It was a time when I felt especially un-humble, un-charitable, un-optimistic, and not particularly proud of my Catholic heritage.

I considered why. It was first and foremost a time of spiritual isolation. A time of stark economic pursuit when academic survival often came at the expense of healthy relationships. It was a time when I found myself moving in circles where words like "grace" and "holiness" and "prayer," words that had sustained me since my youth, earned cynical jeers and sarcastic put-downs.

The environment I have just described is not that dissimilar to the "American mainstream" in which much of the laity today must live and work. Call it the loneliness of a long-distance runner or the exhaustion of a battle-weary warrior, but the Christian's call to be "*in* the world but not *of* it" can be a painful, disheartening walk if faced alone.

My thoughts naturally return to the "Mystical Body of Christ." Isn't this what He had in mind when He asked us to "love one another as I have loved you"? (Jn 15:12) Isn't this what He envisioned when He blessed Simon Peter and gave him "the keys of the kingdom of heaven" (Mt 16:19) at the very moment He formed His Church?

I believe so. For a compassionate faith community offering mutual encouragement and support can ignite a spiritual energy that is irresistible to even the most tarnished and weary souls. In this grace-filled environment, humility, charity, optimism, and legitimate pride can be fostered and will inspire the dedicated servant-leaders we will need among the laity in order to reform the mainstream of American life.

Before leaving these four calls to conscience, I believe that it would be worthwhile to take a moment to also share the origin of my "turning point," the source of my own reawakening to grace. It came in the form of an autobiography written by Dag Hammarskjöld. In his book, *Markings*, he writes in his disarmingly candid style, "If only I can become *firmer, simpler, quieter* and *warmer.*"

I am still not sure if it was the inherent wisdom of what he wrote or the fact that it came from him, the former Secretary General of the United Nations, but somehow I felt less alone as I read his words.

He, too, was struggling with being "in the world but not of it." He, too, was battling the same demons of moral weakness, intellectual complexity, temporal distraction, and emotional rigidity. What's more, he was willing to admit it. More importantly, he was determined to overcome these temptations. In one simple phrase, Dag Hammarskjöld had put into practice the four principles of humility, charity, optimism, and legitimate pride that the Catholic Campaign is recommending to us.

His example was contagious for me then and it can be for us today. My prayer is that the parallels between Hammarskjöld's *"firmer"* and the Campaign's *"legitimate pride,"* between his *"simpler"* and our *"humility,"* between his *"quieter"* and our *"optimism,"* between his *"warmer"* and our *"charity"* might heal us this evening just as these ideas healed me fifteen years ago.

These principles were also addressed time and time again by the Head of our Mystical Body who, after all, had faced a few wilderness experiences of His own. He knew first-hand the agony of Gethsemane. He had personally tasted the bitterness of Thomas' doubt. He had felt the sting of a crowd's mockery even as He hung dying on a cross.

And so He speaks with profound empathy when He detects our faltering humility and reminds us that "the last will be first, and the first last." (Mt 20:16) When he senses our waning *charity*, He implores us to love our enemies (cf. Lk 6:27), and He reminds us "as you did it to one of the least of these . . . you did it to me." (Mt 25:40) When He notes our *pride* in our Church and our faith is weakening, He tenderly refers to His Church as His "bride" and asks us to "Let your light so shine before men, that they may see your good works and give glory to your Father who is in heaven." (Mt 5:16) When He feels our *optimism* being shaken, He promises not to leave us orphans and reassures us, "and lo, I am with you always, to the close of the age." (Mt 28:20)

Conclusion

I write to you not by virtue of any special expertise — but rather because of my role as a fellow pilgrim. Like you, I am keenly aware of the times and the ways that I have failed to live up to the Ten Commandments, let alone the Ten Principles of effective lay witness. But also, like you, I am encouraged by the fact that we are gathered here together at a conference whose purpose is to clarify, unify, and strengthen our voice.

In closing, I'd like to borrow the key words in the ten principles that have taken on much deeper meaning for me:

1) I have never felt more *optimistic* that a resurgence of *hope* is now possible and that it, in turn, will give us all the *courage* necessary to *engage the present culture*.
2) I have never felt more *proud* of my Church, nor more *humbled* by the *faith* of its laity, as I see already in practice the kind of *personal responsibility* that will demand nothing less than becoming *more knowledgeable* about our faith in the years ahead.
3) And finally, I have never felt more *charity* as I see unfolding the kind of *loyalty* that can only grow from genuine *love* . . . a love that will surely be *integrated into every dimension of our lives*.

As this faith, hope, and love are nurtured in and through our collective participation in a revitalized Mystical Body, we have every reason to believe that we, the laity, will be further empowered by the Holy Spirit to "renew the face of the earth."

May the Peace that surpasses all understanding lift your spirit and strengthen your voice so that when we meet again, our Lord might whisper, "Well done, good and faithful servants."

The Rediscovery of Our
American Catholic Heritage

Just over one hundred years ago, in November 1889, our forebears in the faith met in Baltimore for the first Lay Congress, to celebrate the first one hundred years of the nation's first diocese in America, whose first Archbishop was that great friend of George Washington and lover of this Republic, John Carroll.

The mood of that first Lay Congress was ebullient. Proud of what the Catholic people had accomplished in one hundred years, they looked forward with enthusiasm to the next one hundred. They reminded themselves that, in 1776, when John Carroll had accompanied Benjamin Franklin to Canada on a diplomatic mission crucial to the new republic, the nation's Catholic population numbered 25,000. They recalled that during the Revolutionary War, the armed forces were, for the first time, open to Catholic officers, and that many had risen rapidly in the ranks. No citizens, they recalled, were more in favor of the new republic. It was said at the time, one speaker reminded them, that "every Catholic was a Whig" — that is, not a Tory, but positively in favor of the truths enunciated in the Declaration of Independence.

By 1789, when John Carroll was consecrated America's first bishop, Catholics numbered 32,000. One hundred years later, in 1889, they numbered nine million. This one archdiocese had grown into 13, and where there had been one bishop there now were 71, presiding over 8,000 priests and 10,500 churches and chapels, 27 seminaries, 650 colleges and academies of higher education, 3,100 parish schools, and 520 hospitals and asylums.

Pope Leo XIII was delighted with the great events in Baltimore in 1889 — the Lay Congress and the founding of Catholic University — and sent tangible signs of his special love for this country. He had received a beautifully bound copy of the U.S. Constitution from President Grover Cleveland for his fiftieth anniversary in the priesthood, and on receiving it said to its bearer, Archbishop Patrick John Ryan:

> As an Archbishop you enjoy in America perfect freedom. That freedom, we admit, is highly beneficial to the spread of religion. . . . Toward America I bear a special love. . . Your government is free, your future full of hope. Your President commands my highest admiration.

Leo XIII also wrote to Cardinal Gibbons:

> We desire that you should assure the President of our admiration for the Constitution of the United States, not only because it enables industrious and enterprising citizens to attain so high a level of prosperity, but also because under its protection your countrymen have enjoyed a liberty which has so confessedly promoted the astonishing growth of religion in the past and will, we trust, enable it in the future to be of the highest advantage to the civil order as well.

"To be of the highest advantage to the civil order as well. . . ." These words of Leo XIII point to one of the major themes of the great leaders of the American Catholic people, from Archbishop Carroll to Cardinal

Gibbons, from Archbishops Ireland and Ryan and Keane to Bishops such as England and Spalding, from the layman Orestes Brownson to the priest Isaac Hecker. Do not overlook that Greek name "Orestes" and that Judaic name "Isaac"; Americans in those days knew well that they were part of a long and great Tradition, which Chesterton called "the democracy of the dead." Such leaders saw something new and special in this blessed country, under the sweet sway of its institutions, something of great importance to the rest of the world and especially the Catholic world.

Our forebears believed profoundly that Providence had held back this nation from the stage of history until its appointed time, for a destiny that would change the direction of the entire world. Here would be built, under Providence, by a people building "better than they knew " a new civilization of love, under the American name *Philadelphia*, a "city on the hill," a nation conceived in liberty, and dedicated to the proposition that all men are created equal, in conformity with the laws of nature and nature's God. They believed such things as these; let me quote from Isaac Hecker:

> The more a civilization solicits the exercise of man's intelligence and enlarges the field for the action of his free will, the broader will be the basis it offers for sanctity. Ignorance and weakness are the negation of life; they are either sinful or the consequences of sin, and to remedy these common evils is the aim of the Christian religion. Enlightened intelligence and true liberty of the will are the essential conditions of all moral action. . . .

This "enlightened intelligence and true liberty of

the will," Hecker preached, come to humans in their fullness only through the grace of Christ.

Therefore, our forebears wished to bring the whole nation to Christ, in God's good time, and by the example and persuasion of argument rooted in godly lives. As Hecker told the Second Plenary Council of Baltimore in 1866, just after the carnage of the Civil War (a war that deeply divided this city):

> Nowhere is there a promise of a brighter future for the Church than in our own country. Here, thanks to our American Constitution, the church is free to do her divine work. Here she finds a civilization in harmony with divine teachings. Here Christianity is promised a reception from an intelligent and free people, that she will give forth a development of unprecedented glory. For religion is never so beautiful as when in connection with knowledge and freedom. Let us, therefore, arise and open our eyes to the bright future that is before us! Let us labor with a lively faith, a firm hope, and a charity that knows no bounds, by every good work and good example, for the reign of God's Kingdom upon the earth.

It is ennobling for us to recall our American Catholic national leadership of 1789 and 1889. Archbishop Ireland told that first Lay Congress over one hundred years ago: "The past our fathers wrought; the future will be wrought by us. The next century in the life of the Church will be what we make it." At the Third Plenary Council of Baltimore, the bishops of the United States asserted that this country was well-founded, that, under Providence, the framers had "built better than they knew." Their attitude toward the nation was open, optimistic, eager to engage with it and all its citizens.

For they believed, as the French statesman and author Tocqueville believed, that the Republic was not adequate to its own defense; that one day the Catholic people would be the surest guarantors of the "truths" that Jefferson had enunciated in the Declaration and on which our Constitution rests: That there is a Creator Who gave us life and at the same time liberty; that there are truths to be held, anchored in the hard evidence of His creation; that the human intellect is made to seek, to know, and to love the truth, and the truth alone; that humans, although sinful, weak, and often erring, are capable of sober reflection, calm deliberation, and a dispassionate openness to evidence and to reason; that God has promised us eternal life, in whose light every single woman and man, made in the image of their loving Creator, is of priceless value, "immortal diamond," on which account she and he are endowed with inalienable rights directly by the Creator, and not by any state or any contrivance of human will.

American institutions require all these beliefs. But who can defend these beliefs today? Relativists cannot. Those who appeal merely to the Scriptures cannot, if they renounce the way of reason and intellectual inquiry. In a profound sense, atheists and agnostics cannot, although they may argue on Hobbesian grounds that American institutions are the only practicable defense against one another's uncheckable ferocity of will: *homo homini lupus*.

For it is one of the ironies of the end of this century that the carriers of the Enlightenment no longer hold that the intellect has purchase on reality, or can discover intellectual foundations for the "truths we hold." The heirs of the Enlightenment have retreated to subjective preference and the will. They do not claim to hold to the American proposition because it is true, well-founded, or even self-evident (other things being held in mind); rather, they "like" American institutions, they "prefer" American institutions.

Survival of the Self

Under threat, however, will they prefer instead their own survival? Will they buckle under superior force? Many of them now buckle merely under the regime of "political correctness," at the mere hint of arousing the verbal insults of the feminists on campus. What would they do if they had more to fear than words and names? Preference and will provide no defense of truth. Their highest guide is, and must be, the comfortable survival of the self — with which moral abdication is entirely consistent.

The Enlightenment is dead. It has lost its moral fibre. It has lost the protective underpinning it long pretended not to recognize: the belief that the blooming, buzzing confusion of existence is intelligible, as if from the point of view of a single all-mastering intelligence. This is, after all, the suppressed assumption behind all forms of rationalism, whether logical or empirical.

The Enlightenment always was intellectually dependent on Judaism and Christianity, even when it was trying to destroy Judaism and Christianity. It was a child that wished to murder its parents, while pleading, as in Bertrand Russell's *Mysticism and Logic*, that it is a lonely orphan, pathetic in the empty cosmos. The Enlightenment was always rooted in *chutzpa*. And in bigotry: Has any other intellectual movement in history had the arrogance to claim, in the name of open-minded reason, to represent "Enlightenment" (with a capital E) while consigning those not in its party to "the Dark Ages"? Into outer Darkness go ye, who dare to disagree. Pure, inflammatory bigotry.

Nietzsche called the bluff of the Enlightenment. If God is dead, so is Reason.

Thus we live today in the ironic circumstance that the philosophers no longer believe either in God or in Reason. Author and philosopher Richard Rorty smilingly insists: "There is nothing but contingency all the way down." Dizzying nothingness. Vertigo. The only ground Rorty claims to stand on is that of the bourgeois comfort he experiences, and prefers.

The Wrong Moral Track

Poll after poll of the opinions of our people today shows that a strong majority believe that the nation "is on the wrong track." Given the nation's emergence from recession well before the election of 1992, well in advance of other nations, I do not think the people mean "on the wrong economic track." Given that the popular criticisms of our nation's political class always demand greater accountability, I do not think that the people mean "on the wrong political track" — that is, that the democratic republic is a bad idea. The people are saying, rather, that the politicians need to be reined in by the will of the people.

Thus, the most likely interpretation of "on the wrong track" is neither economic nor political. It is moral: Our people hold that the nation is on a wrong *moral* track. They have come to fear that we may not be as good a people as our grandparents were. We do not have their morals. We do not have their virtues. We do not have their character. We are a morally emptier people.

This nation has faced many deadly crises that might have brought an end to our national experiment in self-government: The Revolution could have failed. The Civil War could have split the country, eventually, into at least as many nations as Europe today. The First World War, the Second, or the Cold War might have ended in our defeat. The Depression might have blown the country asunder in bitter class war. During these great struggles, even if the threats they faced threatened to be overwhelming, our people had confidence in their own character — they knew they would give it their best shot, you could count on it.

Today, however, for the first time in American history, no great threats from outside are in evidence: We are afraid of our own moral weaknesses. We are no longer sure that we can rely upon our own character, or even upon the help of a favorable God, whose eye could look upon us with pleasure. We do not fear that God has broken His covenant with us. We have reason to fear that we have broken our covenant with Him.

No one ever guaranteed that America's national experiment will endure forever. It might cross through the skies like a comet that lasted a little over two hundred years, and then went out. "The price of liberty," our founders used to say, "is everlasting vigilance." A regime based on liberty is the most fragile form of regime. The problem with an experiment in liberty is that a single generation, finding it too difficult, might decide one day to give up on it. Last one out, turn out the lights.

I do not think we have the optimism of our

forebears in 1889. One hundred years after that Lay
Congress, we have reason to fear for the future of this
Republic. And fear for it, precisely, on moral and
intellectual grounds. Intellectually, morally, our nation
is on the wrong track. On our campuses, in our movie
industry, on our television talk shows and sitcoms, in
our law schools, in our courts, in our newspapers and
newsweeklies, in our gay bars and our frenetically busy
abortion clinics (slicing to death or killing with acid 1.5
million helpless citizens per year), we have witnessed
an aggressive hostility to Judaism and Christianity —
to any source of transcendent judgment — a hostility
unprecedented in our national experience.

What is dismaying in America today is not the
private striving and private virtue of ordinary mothers
and fathers of families, grandparents, uncles and aunts
and cousins. It is the corrupt *public ethos* — the public
ecology — that is poisoning our public spaces. This
invisible poisonous gas emanates from television sets in
our private homes, it enters through virtually all the
media. The moral air we breathe these days is foul. The
moral ecology of our nation is more polluted than our
cities. Our physical environment is cleaner.

We have barely learned how to think about such
things. We are going to have to learn how to think
about them. More than once in our history, our nation
has experienced a Great Awakening. Today, too, it
needs one.

Choosing to Obey

Institutions of liberty cannot survive in any moral
ecology at all. And neither can our faith. Here, private
life and public life need one another. Every time we

strike a blow for conversion in our private lives, we make more credible a larger conversion in our public life. Every small act of charity is connected to every other by a billion tiny threads. Acts of love circle the globe with the speed of light. A smile offered to another person circles the planet in less than a day. Our task is to work at knitting together this network of charity, these glowing filaments of love and generosity, through scores of random acts of generosity a day. Our task is to insist publicly upon a recognition of the deepest bases of our lives together: a dispassionate commitment to the evidence of truth, since only truth makes us free; a respect for the "immortal diamond" of every person, since our immortality is the ground of the infinite value and inalienable rights of each; and a joyful love of *choosing* to do what we ought to do, that is, the joy of obeying freely the law that our Creator wrote into our nature.

For, as our forebears saw, human beings are the only creatures who do not obey the law of their own nature by instinct, but by choice. The American idea of liberty was always twofold, as Tocqueville pointed out in the first twenty pages of *Democracy in America*: Human liberty is not the same as animal liberty. Animals cannot help obeying the law of their own natures. Animals do what they do by instinct. Humans alone have the choice of doing what they ought to do — or not. Human liberty is not doing what we wish, it is doing what we ought.

All this the French liberal party caught in their design of the Lady of New York harbor, the Statue of Liberty. In her right hand they put the torch of Reason, against the mists of passion, bigotry, and ignorance. In her left hand, they put the Book of the Law. This Lady symbolizes what Pope John Paul II, in his first visit to these shores, called the great American contribution to world civilization, the conception of "ordered liberty." Liberty under Reason. Liberty under the Law. This concept is reflected in a great patriotic hymn:

> Confirm thy soul in self-control
> Thy liberty in law.

To be a citizen of this nation — and even more, to be a Catholic — is to have received much. In another verse, that hymn conveys a classical Catholic conception — that everything we have has been received:

> America, America
> God shed His grace on thee.
>
> And crown thy good with brotherhood
> From sea to shining sea.

It is wonderful to belong to a country that appeals not only to Reason, and not only to Law, but to God's all-encompassing love. Sinners that we are, unworthy of that love, we need often to give thanks. For our country. Above all, for our faith.

And, as we have learned today, there is a lot for us to do. The past, our fathers made. The future, we must make.

Index

OUR
SUNDAY
VISITOR
BOOKS

☰ BEST SELLING BOOKS

CURRENT

Essentials of the Faith:..740-9.......$ 9.95
A Guide to the Catechism of the Catholic Church
By Alfred McBride, O.Praem.

Pontiffs: Popes Who Shaped History ....479-5.......$16.95
By John Jay Hughes

A Pastor's Challenge:......................(cloth)..............738-7.......$19.95
Parish Leadership in an Age of Division,
Doubt, and Spiritual Hunger
By George A. Kelly

Marvels of Charity: ....(cloth)..............648-8.......$29.95
History of American Sisters and Nuns
By George C. Stewart, Jr.

Making Things Right: ....(English)............351-9.......$ 3.95
The Sacrament of Reconciliation ....(Spanish)............349-7 ......$ 3.95
By Jeannine Timko Leichner

Daily Roman Missal......................(bonded leather)......120-6.......$59.95

Exploring The Teaching of Christ..............................624-0.......$139.95
By Bishop Donald W. Wuerl

The Eager Reader Bible Story Book ....(cloth)..............252-0.......$15.95
Catholic Edition

A Guide to the Catechism of................(blackline masters)....126-5.......$29.95
the Catholic Church
By Alfred McBride, O.Praem.

Called to Serve: A Guidebook for............(pkg. of 6)...........663-1.......$14.95
Altar Servers - Revised Edition
By Albert J. Nevins, M.M.

Lives of the Saints You Should Know ....576-7.......$ 7.95
By Margaret and Matthew Bunson

The Catholic One Year Bible (NRSV).........(cloth)..............231-8.......$24.95
....(kivar) ....232-6 ......$18.95

Available at your local religious bookstore or use this page for ordering:
OUR SUNDAY VISITOR • 200 NOLL PLAZA • HUNTINGTON, IN 46750
Please send me the above title(s). I am enclosing payment plus
$3.95 per order to cover shipping/handling. Or, MasterCard/Visa customers
can order by phone **1-800-348-2440**.

Name _____

Address_____

City _____State _____Zip _____

Telephone ( ) _____

Prices and availability subject to change without notice.